PAUL BEHAVING Badly

WAS THE APOSTLE A RACIST, CHAUVINIST JERK?

E. RANDOLPH RICHARDS
and BRANDON J. O'BRIEN

An imprint of InterVarsity Press
Downers Grove, Illinois

InterVarsity Press
P.O. Box 1400, Downers Grove, IL 60515-1426
ivpress.com
email@ivpress.com

InterVarsity Press® is the book-publishing division of InterVarsity Christian Fellowship/USA®, a movement of students and faculty active on campus at hundreds of universities, colleges and schools of nursing in the United States of America, and a member movement of the International Fellowship of Evangelical Students. For information about local and regional activities, visit intervarsity.org.

Cover design: David Fassett
Interior design: Beth McGill
Images: St Paul by Philippos Goul at Church of St. Mamas, Louvaras, Cyprus/Sonia Halliday Photographs/Bridgeman Images

ISBN 978-0-8308-4472-2 (print)
ISBN 978-0-8308-7332-6 (digital)

Printed in the United States of America ♾

As a member of the Green Press Initiative, InterVarsity Press is committed to protecting the environment and to the responsible use of natural resources. To learn more, visit greenpressinitiative.org.

Library of Congress Cataloging-in-Publication Data
A catalog record for this book is available from the Library of Congress.

P 20 19 18 17 16 15 14 13 12 11 10 9 8 7 6 5 4 3 2
Y 33 32 31 30 29 28 27 26 25 24 23 22 21 20 19 18 17 16

"Was Paul a racist? A sexist? A homophobe? Just kind of a jerk? Modern readers are often offended by the apostle's strong words and apparently politically incorrect views. Richards and O'Brien do not sugarcoat or shy away from these issues. Instead, they dig deep into the first-century world to understand Paul on his own terms and in terms of the cultures in which he lived. The result is a deeper understanding of the radical impact of the gospel that Paul preached. This is a great book, full of clarity, nuance, and insight."

Mark L. Strauss, university professor of New Testament, Bethel Seminary, San Diego

"I often hear people say, 'The apostle Paul was a sexist, homophobic bigot, so who cares what he thinks?' Well, Randy Richards and Brandon O'Brien care what he thinks, and they want to make sure that we get a proper picture of Paul, warts and all! They show that while Paul is much maligned, he is little understood, and they act like an attorney cross-examining the controversial apostle on scintillating topics like slavery, women, and homosexuality to get to the bottom of the issues. This is no whitewash; it is an honest grappling with one of the most controversial figures of Western religious history. Whether you love Paul or despise him, you'll never see him the same way again after reading this book!"

Michael F. Bird, lecturer in theology, Ridley College, Melbourne

"In *Paul Behaving Badly,* Richards and O'Brien take up modern charges of racism, sexism, bigotry, and hypocrisy against the apostle Paul. With humility, candor, and not a little wit, these authors present well-reasoned judgments about the apostle's character, ministry, and teachings. As trustworthy guides, Richards and O'Brien show how Paul challenges the cultural and theological issues of his day—and our own. Readers beware: you will be uncomfortable at times, even offended, for Paul's gospel message challenges us all to reexamine our priorities and actions. A must-read for those who teach and preach on Paul, and for all who have questions about the complex apostle."

Lynn H. Cohick, professor of New Testament, Wheaton College

"Like *Jesus Behaving Badly,* this book helpfully responds to many of the misconceptions people have about a key figure in the forming of our faith. In easy-to-understand and engaging language, it explores how Paul related to the setting in which he lived and wrote."

Craig S. Keener, F. M. and Ada Thompson Professor of Biblical Studies, Asbury Seminary

"For those who have been daunted, angered, confused or shocked by the apostle Paul, this fine, honest, lucid book by Richards and O'Brien helps readers better understand Paul in his own first-century setting. The authors do not fully exonerate Paul (he too was finite and sinful), nor do they engage in chronological snobbery, as many of Paul's critics are wont to do ('It's a good thing we moderns know better than Paul'). *Paul Behaving Badly* gives a fresh glimpse into the life and thought of the controversial apostle—one that is both fair minded and charitable, at once challenging to staid assumptions while faithful to Christian orthodoxy."

Paul Copan, professor and Pledger Family Chair of Philosophy and Ethics, Palm Beach Atlantic University, West Palm Beach, Florida

"Richards and O'Brien offer the latest installment in IVP's Behaving Badly books. Unlike when God or Jesus seems to behave badly, we need not exonerate Paul of everything he did, even when it is narrated in Scripture. The stakes are higher with what he taught, however. Our authors show that Paul's teaching surpassed the quality of his peers, even if he didn't go all the way toward certain positions we might wish he held. This is an easy-to-read, judicious guide to responding to Paul's apparent misogyny, homophobia, Scripture-twisting, hypocrisy and more. In some instances, there are other credible options as well, but Richards and O'Brien always give us defensible options. Highly recommended for all who are troubled about these issues or who want to help those who are troubled about them."

Craig L. Blomberg, distinguished professor of New Testament, Denver Seminary

"Paul spent much of his ministry under attack. Nearly two thousand years later, the arrows are still flying. Patriarchal, racist, braggadocious, mercurial, the dark genius who corrupted the pure message of Jesus—he's been accused of it all. Even Christians have a tendency to look askance at the brash apostle when his words grate on our modern sensibilities. *Paul Behaving Badly* is a defense of the apostle that strikes just the right tone. Richards and O'Brien account for the understandable objections people have to Paul's writings while gently correcting misunderstandings. This learned and readable work will resonate with fans and foes of the embattled apostle and illuminate Paul's passion for the gospel and the Christ it proclaims. I can't imagine a more needed book on a more important topic."

Drew Dyck, senior editor, CTpastors.com, author of *Yawning at Tigers*

For my daughter-in-law, Anastasha Richards

For my daughter, Eliza O’Brien

CONTENTS

PREFACE

When our wonderful editor and friend, Dr. Al Hsu, approached us about writing *Paul Behaving Badly,* we were excited. This should be easy. What could go wrong? Two fine books have been written in recent years that are similar to this one: *God Behaving Badly* by David Lamb and *Jesus Behaving Badly* by Mark Strauss. The way has been paved for us. We just have to walk in it.

Then it occurred to us that Paul wasn't God or Jesus. Obviously. More to the point, Jesus was perfect and God is, well, God. But Paul was a mortal human. He was the one who wrote: "I do not understand what I do. For what I want to do I do not do, but what I hate I do" (Rom 7:15). Before you even begin reading the other two books, you feel somehow that everything is going to be okay. Surely neither God nor Jesus ever really behaved badly, right? But it is very possible that Paul did. After all, he's only human.

We encourage you to stay with us while we investigate the case against Paul. We ask that you trust us. We love God's Holy Word and believe it to be 100 percent true. We also believe that the Bible will stand up to a good hard look and thorough investigation.

Because we hold these convictions, we do our best to make compelling arguments *against* Paul in every chapter. Some may feel we've been unfair to him or that we're abusing Scripture or being irreverent. We assure you that our motives are pure. Bear with us. When it is done, we think you'll be satisfied.

We (Randy and Brandon) represent different generations but we both grew up in the evangelical church. While it is en vogue these days to bash the church for all it gets wrong, we were and are deeply blessed by faithful men and women who taught us to love God and revere his Word. We both have dedicated our lives to teaching the Bible and theology to the next generation of believers. Randy has been teaching since 1988 in evangelical colleges in Texas, Indonesia, Arkansas and now Florida. Brandon, a younger scholar, has been an editor and writer since 2007 and has taught in universities in Illinois and Arkansas. We both currently teach Bible and theology in colleges that hold a high view of Scripture. Both of us have served as pastors in churches around the country. This book flows out of our desire to equip Christians who don't have extensive biblical or theological training to think critically and faithfully about the Scriptures and their meaning for us in the twenty-first century.

This is our second book together. *Misreading Scripture with Western Eyes* was our first attempt to bring current scholarly research into conversation with issues of interest to Christians outside the academy. We hope we have had the same success in this volume. In both of our books, we include personal stories because we are convinced stories communicate truth. But this book isn't about us; it's about Paul—that brash, bold apostle to the Gentiles.

Introduction

THE PROBLEMS WITH PAUL

The apostle Paul spent a lot of time defending himself in court and evading arrest. He was hauled before the Roman authorities on several occasions for behaving badly—for disrupting temples and fomenting unrest, charges taken very seriously in the first century. Three times (that we know of) Jewish leaders hatched a plot to assassinate Paul for speaking against the temple in Jerusalem or against the law of Moses. On at least one occasion, Jews and Gentiles plotted *together* to snuff out Paul (Acts 14:1-7). Jews and Gentiles didn't often see eye to eye, but apparently members of both groups considered the apostle from Tarsus a menace that needed to be silenced. Paul summarizes a few other instances when he faced disciplinary action for his bad behavior:

> Five times I received from the Jews the forty lashes minus one. Three times I was beaten with rods, once I was pelted with stones. . . . I have been constantly on the move. I have been in danger . . . from my fellow Jews, in danger from Gentiles; . . . and in danger from false believers. (2 Cor 11:24-26)

We might find this record of abuses admirable if we didn't have the nagging feeling that Paul brought some of it on himself. Sure, the Jewish leaders also plotted to have Jesus executed, but when Jesus appeared before Pilate there was "no basis for a charge against him" (Jn 18:38). It is true the twelve disciples are all said to have died martyrs' deaths at the hands of Gentiles, but they managed to preach and teach until the end of their lives without being constantly harassed by Jewish officials. In other words, Paul has the dubious distinction among the earliest Christians of irritating *everyone* at some point—and sometimes everyone all at once. Persecution can be the consequence of faithfulness, but it can also be evidence of orneriness.

I (Brandon) understand where Paul's opponents were coming from. There was a time while I was in college that I didn't much care for the apostle Paul. I believed his writings were Scripture, that they were true and divinely inspired, so I didn't question whether Paul was right about the theology he propounded. But, boy, did he rub me the wrong way. He struck me as arrogant about his superior spirituality. "If someone else thinks they have reasons to put confidence in the flesh," Paul wrote to the Philippians, "I have more." He considered himself "a Hebrew of Hebrews" and, "as for righteousness based on the law, faultless" (Phil 3:4-5). Want to know how to live the Christian life successfully? "Follow my example" (1 Cor 11:1) and "become like me" (Gal 4:12). Goodness. Aren't we called "Christ followers" and not "Paul followers"? In the words of Paul, I heard the arrogance of a handful of church leaders I knew, each of them insisting they were "God's man" and that their opinions were therefore divinely inspired. *Disagree with me,* I could easily imagine Paul saying, *and you're disagreeing with God.*

Paul also had a way of belittling folks that made me bristle. He called the believers in Galatia "foolish" (Gal 3:1). In the same letter he even boasted about confronting a brother publicly: "When Cephas [Peter] came to Antioch, I opposed him to his face, because he stood condemned" (Gal 2:11). And this from a Christian man who commanded another group of believers: "As far as it depends on you, live at peace with everyone" (Rom 12:18). I found it difficult to harmonize the example of Paul with the example of Jesus. Where Jesus said, "Come to me, all you who are weary and burdened, and I will give you rest" (Mt 11:28), Paul said, "Expel the wicked person from among you!" (1 Cor 5:13). Where Jesus said, "Turn . . . the other cheek" (Mt 5:39), Paul said that if anyone disagreed with him, "Let them be under God's curse" (Gal 1:8-9).

Reading Paul, it was hard to imagine myself as a faithful Christian if *he* was the model of faithful Christianity. None of that confrontation and bravado is in my constitution. I didn't denounce Paul, but I sure didn't like him.

I (Randy) had other problems with Paul. He intimidated me. I wouldn't admit it, but I just preferred to study John. John seemed simpler. I didn't find John confusing. I certainly agreed with Peter when he said that Paul's letters "contain some things that are hard to understand" (2 Pet 3:16). When I entered PhD studies on the New Testament, I avoided taking any courses on Paul for as long as I could because Paul said that we aren't under the law, but then he used the law to make his point. Understanding Paul was *hard*.

Matters became more complicated for each of us when, deeper into our theological studies, we discovered that there is no shortage of people who totally reject Paul's perspective on the Christian life. We thought Paul was arrogant, but others believed he was a misogynist and that his view of women was responsible for generations of gender inequality and the patriarchal subjugation of wives and daughters. We thought he was insensitive, but others considered him a racist and anti-Semite. The charge certainly seemed to stick since Christians have quoted Paul to justify their persecution of Jews and the enslavement of Africans and their descendants in America. We felt he failed to embody the meekness and gentleness of Jesus. Others claimed he had invented Christianity. Jesus went around preaching, "The kingdom of heaven is near." Paul preached about blood and faith and resurrection. Some learned critics argued Paul's emphasis on sin and atonement departed radically from Jesus' simple gospel of peace and forgiveness. Not only that, they claim, but this departure from Jesus' teaching was no accident. The preeminent Jesus scholar Albert Schweitzer wrote of Paul, "If we had to rely on Paul, we should not know that Jesus taught in parables, had delivered the Sermon on the Mount, and had taught His disciples the 'Our Father.' Even where they are specially relevant, *Paul passes over the words of the Lord*."[1]

One critic of Paul's has argued that Paul reinforces the dominant, middle-class values of Western society, whereas Jesus' teaching is too radical for most to appreciate:

> Unlike Jesus of Nazareth, however, who was a Liberal who built up the weak and the poor, while tearing down the mighty, Paul of Tarsus was a Conservative who did a great deal of putting down the weak: women, slaves, Jews, homosexuals and the poor, while empowering those in power. . . . Paul has proven himself the dream theologian of Conservatives, who for centuries has provided them any number of bible passages to help white, European, male, prosperous, heterosexual "Christians" keep the rest of mankind under their feet.[2]

It seems to us these charges go too far. Our distaste for Paul's personality did not pose any real threat to our Christian faith. But is it possible to dismiss all these charges as merely issues of Paul's personality? After all, he *does* tell wives to submit to their husbands and slaves to obey their masters (Eph 5–6). That seems anti-woman and pro-slavery. Paul *does* say the Jews killed Jesus, that "they displease God and are hostile to everyone" (1 Thess 2:15). That certainly seems anti-Semitic. But if you believe, as we do, that Paul's writings are God-breathed, then acknowledging that Paul thought poorly of women means acknowledging that God thinks poorly of women; admitting Paul was a racist means admitting that God is a racist; believing that Paul and Jesus preached two different gospels implies that God inspired two different gospels. We are not willing to agree to those things.

We are, however, willing to admit that the charges against Paul have merit. We cannot merely harrumph and dismiss charges of immorality, misogyny and racism as trivial. So what we propose to do in the remainder of this book is to put Paul on trial as people have done for two thousand years. Each chapter compiles the common charges against Paul—that he was rude and arrogant, a chauvinist and racist, a prude and a homophobe, a hypocrite and a twister of Scripture. We have collected the evidence and make the case against Paul on all the charges as ardently and honestly as we can. It turns out these charges aren't empty slander. Then we switch sides. We take the charges seriously by responding reasonably and not being dismissive. Specifically, we mine Paul's historical and cultural context in an effort to hear what he has to say and interpret what he means in a way that would make sense to his original audience. But this exercise isn't as straightforward as it may seem.

THE CHALLENGE OF INTERPRETATION

One of the challenges of interpreting Paul is that his writings are what scholars call "occasional writings." That doesn't mean that Paul only wrote periodically. It means that when he wrote, it was with a specific audience and situation in mind. His writings were specific to a particular occasion (hence, "occasional"). This wouldn't necessarily pose a problem for us if we had all the information to reconstruct the occasions for which Paul wrote. If we knew, for example, what questions people had asked him, what crises he was responding to, what books were on his desk when he penned his thoughts, well, the work would be half done for us. Unfortunately, we don't have access to all that information.

What we have to work with are Paul's letters compiled in the New Testament. These letters are *half* a correspondence. In some cases, they are Paul's responses to letters he received from others. But we don't have *their* letters with their questions and concerns, so we're listening in on only one side of a private conversation. We don't know the exact dates all the letters were composed, so we can't say with absolute confidence what situations or events may have shaped Paul's thoughts on a subject. So then we must weigh all the evidence and make educated guesses. Like all good readers of Paul, we try to recreate the world in which Paul was ministering and writing, and interpret what he had to say in that context.

And, of course, another challenge we face when interpreting Paul is that we bring to the project all our own presuppositions, cultural assumptions and personal baggage. We discovered in the process of writing that Paul is indeed guilty of behaving badly, but not always in the ways one might first imagine. Sometimes it seems Paul is guilty of behaving badly in the eyes of his Jewish, Roman and (broadly speaking) Gentile original audiences. He frequently offended their sensibilities, challenged their assumptions and exposed their misperceptions. We are usually okay with that. Other times, though, Paul appears guilty of behaving badly in the eyes of our contemporary secular culture. We are usually less okay with this. When Paul offends modern sensibilities, breaking our cultural virtues and exemplifying our capital vices, he embarrasses us in front of our cultured friends and family. He becomes the uncle we can't disown but can't in good conscience endorse. And then sometimes Paul is guilty of behaving badly in the eyes of the church, both in his day and ours. It is in these moments that Paul causes us the most grief. Not even his fellow Christians were or are always sure what to make of him.

So, Is Paul's View God's View?

If Paul's letters are inspired—if they are the Word of God—then we can't just sweep them under the rug as "the way the ancients thought." We wouldn't want to dismiss Paul's instructions, but we also recognize that ancients thought differently. God rebukes Job for questioning him when Job doesn't even understand the world around him: Job is ridiculed for not knowing where the earth's footings are (Job 38:6) and for never visiting the storerooms where God keeps the snow (Job 38:22). God's Word also states: "The sun rises and the sun sets, and hurries back to where it rises" (Eccles 1:5). Today, Christians still consider Job and Ecclesiastes to be the Word of God, so we say that God worked within the ancients' understanding of the cosmos. We don't want to find ourselves like the Christians who opposed Galileo, so we allow Job and the ancients to live in their world. We need to allow Paul the same opportunity.

In the pages that follow, we aim to hold Paul's feet to the fire about these important issues. We think he'd approve. Paul admired the Bereans for searching the Scriptures to confirm the truth of his message after they had given him an honest listen (Acts 17:11). In the final assessment, the portrait of Paul that will emerge from this investigation is complex and nuanced. He was a real human being with real emotions and deep convictions. To be perfectly honest, you may not be comfortable with Paul's position even after it's been clarified. You might even react like many of Paul's early Christian hearers. If Paul causes an uproar in your church, it wouldn't be the first time (Acts 15).

Paul in His Time and Ours

In the introduction of nearly every biography, authors note that their subjects were products of their time. The impulse is a good one because it is an effort to take context seriously. If you want to understand someone's motives and the significance of their beliefs or actions, you have to consider them in light of the age and culture in which they acted. That's why so many biographies use "the life and times" in their titles. You can't understand a person without also understanding their context.

In that spirit we should offer a brief overview of Paul's life, but since entire books have been dedicated to that subject, let us instead highlight a few items.[3] Where one was raised is more important than it might seem, for it determines one's heart language and thus one's worldview. Based on the best reading of Acts 22:3, evangelical scholars think Paul was born in Tarsus but raised in Jerusalem. Thus his perspective would be that of a Palestinian Jew, a Judean, and from a family of Pharisees (Acts 23:6). Paul received the highest level of education that traditional Jewish culture allowed, studying under the premier rabbi of the time, Gamaliel (Acts 22:3). He spoke Hebrew and Aramaic, was a rising star in Jerusalem and led the movement opposing Christianity (Acts 22:4).

Having said that, it is unwise to draw too strong a distinction between Palestinian Judaism and the broader Greco-Roman culture. Let's use a modern analogy. Many committed Christians in our churches would assert they are not like the "pagan culture" of general America. In many religious ways, that is true. Yet in many other ways, it is not true. They speak "American" (a dialect of English) and have a general American viewpoint on such things as money, politics ("freedom is worth fighting for"), marriage, careers, leisure and what constitutes the good life. Most of them have the same kind of education as other Americans. Likewise, Paul shared many things in common with the broader culture of his day. He spoke Greek. He used "pagan" money and transportation systems. He likely went to plays and city games.[4] He wrote letters like his contemporaries did. He used Greco-Roman rhetoric and quoted their philosophers (Acts 17:28). He was at home in a typical Roman city, not just with the streets and city layout but also with how government functioned. He was a Roman citizen and probably a member of the tentmakers trade guild.

On the one hand, then, Paul was different—uniquely gifted and called by Christ. On the other hand, he was a first-century Jewish denizen of the Roman Empire. We certainly shouldn't expect him to act like a twenty-first-century American. We all know that Paul was not like us. We should expect him to be a man of *his* time. Nonetheless, determining just what that means is sometimes harder than we think.

That's why a key part of our approach to the subject matter in this book is to dig deeper into Paul's contemporary context. Sometimes, for example, we will be frustrated with Paul because he seems too *conservative* for us—because he's not saying enough about the inherent value of women or slaves. As we get to know Paul's historical context we will discover that his compatriots were often frustrated with him because he was too *progressive* on those issues; he went way further in his support of women and slaves than any of his contemporaries. In short, we will see that Paul is guilty of behaving badly in every age. Even though his opinions do not change with time, our perceptions of them do change.

Now the danger in calling people products of their time is that we risk giving too much credit to the influence of a particular culture. We can't assume that someone's historical context will explain away all his or her behavior. Humans no doubt absorb a great deal of the zeitgeist of their era, but they also are free to transcend it. Adolf Hitler and Mahatma Gandhi were both men of their time—men of the *same* time. It goes without saying that they left quite different legacies behind them. So we may discover after studying a person's historical context that they are even more enigmatic than we imagined. We may discover that Paul, to be specific, is not only out of sync with *our* time, but that he was also out of sync with *his* time. We believe that historical context can tell us a lot about where a person's worldview begins, but it does not necessarily determine where that person's worldview will end. We will appeal to context throughout this book as essential for understanding Paul in his own words, but in the process we will work hard to make sure we allow Paul to be the revolutionary he was. This makes him hard to pin down at times. We think he'd be happy to hear that.

PAUL ON A PEDESTAL

There are those who dislike Paul, who view Paul as so much a product of his time that his opinions are now outdated and outmoded. That whatever value his viewpoint may have had, it has passed its expiration date. They deem him irrelevant and out of step with the times.

However, there are others who think *too highly* of Paul. Western Christians tend to run straight to Paul when they want the "New Testament" answer to a tough question. They don't ask Jesus. They ask Paul.

It is important to remember that Paul is *not* the Son of God. His writings point *to* the Son of God. It is important to remember that while Paul, by divine inspiration, *wrote* the words of God, he was not himself the Word of God. Jesus is alive. Paul is dead (biologically speaking). But too often we elevate Paul to a position of honor just short of where we set Jesus. We believe that Paul's writings are inspired, but we do not believe Paul's personality was inspired. One of our goals in this book is to humanize Paul—to remind us that he was a human being with all the foibles and potentials we all carry.

So with that we invite you to start this journey with us. We ask you to read with an open mind, prepared to better understand one of history's most influential and controversial figures.

one

PAUL WAS KIND OF A JERK

Charles Monroe Sheldon considered Christ the supreme model of Christian behavior. That's why the Topeka pastor wrote the novel *In His Steps* (1896), a story about a minister who challenges his congregants to judge all their actions by first asking themselves, "What would Jesus do?" The title is borrowed from Peter's words in 1 Peter 2:21, and the book is one of the best-selling publications of all time. The subtitle became a popular catchphrase a century later (WWJD) and challenged a new generation of Christians to follow the example of Jesus.

Jesus himself said, "Follow me," so we expect our ministers and mentors to encourage us to be more like Jesus. All of us *should* be more like Jesus. Christians expect the disciples of Jesus to say, as Peter did, "Follow the example of Jesus," but it takes a special kind of chutzpah for a *disciple* to say, "Follow *my* example."

Paul had chutzpah.

"Join together in following *my* example, brothers and sisters," he encourages the Philippians (Phil 3:17, emphasis added). At the very least, he claimed an intermediary role between Jesus and other Christians. "Follow my example," Paul exhorts, "as I follow the example of Christ" (1 Cor 11:1). This from the man who challenges the Romans to "not think of yourself more highly than you ought" (Rom 12:3). It may be that Paul's first-century readers had no problem with this instruction from their spiritual mentor. Maybe it didn't sound brash to people then, but few modern Christians could summon the self-confidence to say these words about their own life: "Follow my example." Coming from someone else, even from the pen of an apostle, the advice sounds arrogant.

In another letter, Paul tells the Galatians that God "set me apart from my mother's womb" (Gal 1:15). We might not blink at that statement. We typically assume that all of us are chosen in our mother's womb, but that's not what Paul meant. The Bible only identifies a handful of people as set apart by God from before birth: Samson, David, Isaiah, Jeremiah, John the Baptist, Jesus. God specially appointed all of them for a specific role in redemptive history. That's what Paul had in mind. He was like those guys. He was exceptional.

Statements like these—*follow my example because I'm exceptional!*—have earned Paul a reputation for being kind of a jerk. The truth is, this is just the beginning. Paul asserted his opinions, even when he was wrong. He bossed around churches and bulldozed other leaders. In 2014, the famed German scholar Gerd Lüdemann noted Paul's "streak of arrogance and a tendency to vacillate," and said Paul's claims of "authority reinforced his sense of infallibility and often led him to bully any who disagreed."[1] While we don't think Paul ever vacillated, he does seem to bully. This description may bring to mind certain celebrity pastors who seem immune to rebuke, or leaders from your past (and ours) who delivered their opinions from on high as if they were speaking the very words of God.

Elsewhere Paul curses his opponents (Gal 1:8). Some people try to rehabilitate Paul's reputation by exclaiming, "I'm sure that's not what he really meant." But that really is what he meant. He repeats it just to make sure we got it: "I say again: If anybody is preaching to you a gospel other than what you accepted, let them be under God's curse!" (Gal 1:9). Paul claims to be superior to many of his contemporaries in keeping Torah (Gal 1:14), claims to speak in tongues more than all the Corinthians combined (1 Cor 14:18) and claims to have worked harder than all the other apostles (1 Cor 15:10). Then he curses some others in Corinth (1 Cor 16:22). Taken in total, his conduct has caused at least one modern Christian to claim, "No Christian genuinely seeking the righteousness of God should imitate a man like Paul."[2]

Apostle to the Gentiles—and Don't You Forget It!

Apostles held special status among the earliest Christians. In the New Testament, the term "apostles" usually designates Jesus' twelve closest disciples. Throughout the Gospels and Acts, this core group is often identified by a collective name: the Twelve (see for example Mt 26:20; Mk 9:35; Lk 9:12; Jn 6:67; Acts 6:2). These men made up Jesus' inner circle, his most intimate friends. To the masses Jesus spoke in parables, but to the Twelve he explained in detail the mysteries of the kingdom of God (Mk 4:10-11). They were the only people who saw Jesus calm the stormy sea, walk on water and break the bread of the Last Supper. Even after Jesus ascended to heaven, the apostles were forever affected by their experience with him in life. Everybody noticed. Even the enemies of the apostles, Israel's leaders who tried to suppress the Gospel, noticed: "When they saw the courage of Peter and John and realized that they were unschooled, ordinary men, they were astonished and they took note that *these men had been with Jesus*" (Acts 4:13, emphasis added). Having been with Jesus marked them as special.

When heresy and schism threatened the unity of the young church in the next generation after all the apostles were dead, church leaders appealed to the authority of the apostles to give church members confidence in their pastors and in the Scriptures. Clement of Rome, one of the first bishops of Rome who was possibly a companion of the apostle Paul (Phil 4:3), argued that the leaders of the local churches could be trusted because they were appointed by the apostles. The pastors were appointed by the apostles, the apostles were appointed by Christ, Christ was sent by God (1 Clement 42:1-4; 44:1-3). In the next couple of generations, "apostolicity" was an important criterion for a book to be considered part of the canon of Scripture. You could trust the content of the books written by folks like Matthew and John because *they had been there*. They had witnessed Jesus' miracles and heard his teaching with their own ears. John himself asserts: "That . . . which we have heard, which we have seen with our eyes, which we have looked at and our hands have touched—this we proclaim concerning the Word of life" (1 Jn 1:1). So the earliest Christians "devoted themselves to the apostles' teaching" (Acts 2:42). Christian tradition inherited its reverence for the apostles from the New Testament itself.

There are times Paul seems not to care about all that. Paul was not one of the Twelve. He did not follow nor interact with Jesus before his crucifixion. Gerd Lüdemann observes, "He did not consider the life of Jesus of Nazareth to be an important topic. Paul never met Jesus personally and had little familiarity with his deeds and teachings."[3] This is overstating the case, though it is true Paul rarely quotes Jesus. And the only sense in which Paul ever spoke with Jesus was on the Damascus road, yet in that interaction Jesus told Paul off. Paul dismisses the fact that the other apostles had walked with Jesus; they knew him "according to the flesh" (2 Cor 5:16 ESV). He never expresses any disappointment that he didn't follow Jesus through the villages of Galilee. Instead he brags about learning at the feet of Gamaliel (Acts 22:3).

Instead of honoring the apostles, Paul insisted that he was just as authoritative as any of them. He says the apostles were "reputed to be pillars" (Gal 2:9 NASB)—an expression not intended to be complimentary. He asserts "I consider myself not in the least inferior to the most eminent apostles" (2 Cor 11:5 NASB). He doesn't consider the apostles' proximity to Jesus to have elevated their status in the least. Luke thought it was important that he had received the message from those who had been there. He was careful to compose a faithful account "just as they were handed down to us by those who from the first were eyewitnesses and servants of the word" (Lk 1:2). It mattered to Luke if you were an eyewitness. It didn't matter to Paul that he wasn't.

Time and again Paul emphasizes that "*his* gospel" is precisely that: his own. "I did not receive it from any man, nor was I taught it" (Gal 1:12). Following his encounter with the risen Jesus on the road to Damascus, Paul's "immediate response was not to consult any human being" (Gal 1:16). When Paul finally interacted with the Christian leaders in Jerusalem a decade later (Gal 2:1), he insists that they "added nothing to my message" (Gal 2:6). How arrogant it seems that Paul would be so unwilling to submit himself to the teaching of the apostles when others did—and on the grounds that he didn't have to because he was an apostle too!

So confident was Paul in his understanding of the gospel that he felt free to challenge the Twelve. Peter, for example, was happy to eat with Gentiles in Antioch. But when "certain men came from James," Peter withdrew from the Gentiles and he influenced other Jews to do the same (Gal 2:12). On the face of it, Peter appears guilty of little more than being cliquish. But Paul lays into him. When he saw that Peter was "not acting in line with the truth of the gospel" (Gal 2:14) Paul "opposed him to his face, because he stood condemned" (Gal 2:11). And he did it "in front of them all" (Gal 2:14). In the process of calling Peter out, he delivers a theological treatise on the law and the gospel. He presumed to correct Peter's gospel—a gospel Peter knew firsthand *because he had walked with Jesus.*

Peter may have been wrong. Like all of us at times, Peter may have momentarily stepped off the path of discipleship. But show

Imagine This

Paul is the newest staff member at the booming five-thousand-member church you started. He wasn't there when the church was planted. He wasn't part of the first meetings in your living room. He never had to load and unload the sound equipment in the hot sun at the rented high school. And yet he is so confident in his opinion that he corrects you publicly on stage and in your face. Or, Paul is the new employee you've hired at your company who has a fancy degree and no experience, but is certain that he's doing it right and you're doing it wrong. I wonder if it bothered Peter to be corrected in front of everyone. It certainly would have irritated me. I don't mind being corrected, but there is a right way to do it and then there is a way that makes you a jerk.

some respect. Peter was there when Jesus was arrested. Peter was there when Jesus fed the five thousand. Peter was the spokesperson at Pentecost. For goodness sake, Peter was chosen to be one of the three to witness the transfiguration! In a storm, Peter walked on water (Mt 14:29); Paul, in a storm, had to swim (Acts 27:42-44). Jesus commanded his disciples, "If your brother sins, go and show him his fault *in private*" (Mt 18:15 NASB, emphasis added). Paul didn't do that. He confronted Peter publicly and to his face. He shamed a highly regarded shepherd of God in front of the flock.

Paul on a Pedestal

Evangelicals often give Paul extra credit and justify his behavior because we have him on a pedestal that is just an inch or two shorter than Jesus. It's an honest temptation since Paul wrote most of the New Testament. Even so, Paul's contemporaries did not share that temptation. Luke, the writer of Acts and occasional traveling companion of Paul, obviously admired Paul but he still went out of his way to remind us that Paul wasn't perfect. Many popular Greco-Roman stories of the day included a "divine-man" character. But Luke wants everyone to know that Paul wasn't half-man, half-god. Paul wasn't Hercules, so Luke tells two stories in which his readers would have immediately recognized that Paul was wrong.

In the first, Paul has a falling out with Barnabas, "a Levite from Cyprus, whom the apostles called Barnabas (which means 'son of encouragement')" (Acts 4:36).

Notice that Luke starts the story by reminding us of Barnabas's excellent pedigree and nickname that all of us would admire. Barnabas was the first disciple to vouch for Paul after Paul's "conversion" from persecutor to propagator of the gospel

(Acts 9:27). In Acts, Barnabas always acts with integrity (Acts 11:22-25). On the second missionary journey, Barnabas wants to take John Mark along. Paul disagrees, because he considers John Mark a quitter (Acts 15:37-38). The disagreement becomes so strong that Barnabas and Paul split. Who was right, Barnabas or Paul? Our instinct might be to justify Paul—he's the hero, right? Not at the time. The first readers of the book of Acts would know John Mark had written a Gospel. Many would know that Mark was a later companion of Paul (Col 4:10; Philem 24) and that Paul considered Mark personally useful (2 Tim 4:11). In other words, while we modern readers give Paul the benefit of the doubt, in the first century that honor would have gone to John Mark and Barnabas. Besides, if you had a problem with Barnabas, *you* were the problem. He was a saint.

Luke records another episode in Acts that illustrates his willingness to point out Paul's faults. It also illustrates an insight into Paul's personality—that being wrong didn't stop Paul from being confident. When Paul wanted to travel to Jerusalem, the Christians in Tyre urged Paul "through the Spirit" not to go to Jerusalem (Acts 21:4). When Paul left Tyre, he traveled *toward Jerusalem* to Caesarea. While he was there, the prophet Agabus received a vision from the Holy Spirit and walked all the way from Judea (thirty miles!) to tell Paul not to go to Jerusalem. The apostles who traveled with Paul to Caesarea told him not to go to Jerusalem. The Caesarean believers told Paul not to go to Jerusalem.

Paul decided to go to Jerusalem. He simply "would not be dissuaded" (Acts 21:14). In his defense, he gave a very spiritual-sounding explanation for ignoring everyone's advice. "I am ready not only to be bound," Paul said, "but also to die in Jerusalem for the name of the Lord Jesus" (Acts 21:13). That's good, because when he arrived in Jerusalem, he was promptly arrested.

Let's avoid letting Paul off the hook on which Luke clearly puts him. Luke was careful with his words. He tells us *Paul said* that the Spirit wanted Paul to go to Jerusalem, and then Luke clearly states that the *Spirit said* otherwise: "Through the Spirit they urged Paul not to go on to Jerusalem" (Acts 21:4). If we want to keep Paul on his pedestal, we must reverse what Luke said. We think Paul was right and the others were wrong, but Luke says the opposite.[4]

The moral of the story is if you think the Holy Spirit is saying one thing and everyone else disagrees—particularly if everyone else includes famous prophets, the Twelve, and all the Christians along the Mediterranean coast—you should at least consider the possibility that you might have misunderstood the Spirit. But Paul, it seems, sometimes trusted his own instincts and interpretations more than those of others. Luke had no problem pointing out Paul's stubbornness and misdirected certainty. We shouldn't gloss over it either.

Pauline Irony: Peace in the Christian Community

By the way we've described Paul so far (which is to say, in his own words), it is difficult to imagine that this confrontational Paul is the same man who exhorted other Christians, "If it is possible, as far as it depends on you, live at peace with everyone" (Rom 12:18). It is difficult to imagine that this obstinate Paul is the same man who urged the believers in Ephesus, "Submit to one another out of reverence for Christ" (Eph 5:21). It is difficult to imagine that the boastful Paul who tirelessly defended his apostleship is the same man who lamented, "For I am the least of the apostles and do not even deserve to be called an apostle, because I persecuted the church of God" (1 Cor 15:9). It would be simple enough to conclude that Paul was merely a hypocrite, that he taught one way and behaved another. (We address that charge in chapter seven.)

Instead, let us suggest that Paul was, like all of us, a complex personality and that he admittedly had a great capacity for stubbornness. Paul received the harshest discipline a synagogue member could receive: thirty-nine lashes. (Synagogue members couldn't be executed, that is, receive forty lashes.) If Paul quit the synagogue, he wouldn't have received the lashes. Yet he accepted the punishment in order to remain a member so he could keep preaching the gospel in synagogues. What's more amazing is that he takes the beating more than once (2 Cor 11:24). Talk about stubborn! The stubbornness that got him into trouble was the same stubbornness that helped him persevere in the face of all manner of hardships.

At the same time that Paul could be stubborn, he also had a great capacity for humility. In Acts 21, just after Paul demonstrates his stubborn resistance to his colleagues' warning not to enter Jerusalem, Paul also demonstrates his willingness to submit to the leadership of other apostles. News about Paul reached Jerusalem before he did. Jewish leaders there, known as "Judaizers," were convinced that Paul had abandoned the law of Moses and that he was encouraging faithful Jews to do the same. The gossip wasn't actually far off the mark. Paul had just written to the Romans: "Christ is the end of the law" (Rom 10:4 NRSV). Nonetheless, the rumors were slanderous, for Paul was accused of teaching apostasy.

So James has a plan to smooth things over and tells Paul to "do what we tell you" (Acts 21:23). Just that bossy tone would have set me off, but James does more. He instructs Paul to join a group of four brothers who have taken a vow. It is unclear the kind of vow because Luke doesn't say. Probably it was a vow to cleanse oneself from the uncleanness of traveling in Gentile lands.[5] The most pious Jews arriving in Jerusalem might undertake such a purification vow. As Craig Keener points out, "Jewish nationalism [was] on the rise" in Paul's day and "nationalism's exclusivity makes it intolerant of supposedly faithful members of its people who have fellowship with members of other peoples."[6] Those Jewish nationalist (anti-Gentile) sentiments were high in Jerusalem at this time, and since Paul had been seen in town with Trophimus the Ephesian—a Gentile (Acts 21:29)—the purification vow was an attempt to appease his opponents.

In any case, the brothers have high fees to pay, and they plan to shave their heads. James suggests Paul should pay their expenses, join them in their purification and shave his head too. This Jewish purification rite would show publicly (by a shaved head) that Paul was keeping Jewish law. It was intended to satisfy Jewish opponents of the gospel who had slandered Paul as a lawbreaker. So why should Paul do what James asks? Paul has always insisted he too is an apostle and not under their authority (but rather Christ's). Paul had no need to purify himself (Rom 14:14). Yet this wasn't a theological debate—Paul never backed down from those. Paul was, in fact, a faithful Jew. James was worried about slander and all it would take to "fix it" was for Paul to humble himself, so Paul complied without objection. "The next day Paul took the men and purified himself along with them" (Acts 21:26). In this way Paul demonstrates beautifully what he has just written to the Romans: "If it is possible, as far as it depends on you, live at peace with everyone" (Rom 12:18). He quite dramatically puts his money where his mouth is.

Taken together, Paul's confronting Peter and submitting to James illuminate an important facet of Paul's personality. Paul was compliant and willing to submit to others if the only thing at stake was his own pride. I'm sure Paul didn't *want* to join the vow or pay the fees for the brothers involved, but he took it on the chin. He refused to allow any obstacle to stand between any person and the gospel, including himself—so he shaved his head.[7] However, if the gospel was at stake, Paul was inflexible. Where eating with Gentiles was concerned, Paul believed Peter's actions would confuse Gentile converts about the nature of the gospel and salvation by faith. If Paul thought someone had the gospel wrong, he refused to back down.

We find this pattern elsewhere in accounts of Paul's ministry. In Philippi, Paul is arrested. News of his arrest would put in question the reputation both of the gospel and of the host, Lydia, who offered her home to Paul and his team. How much confidence would you put in a preacher who was summarily arrested for disturbing the peace? When Paul is released and told to leave town, he first goes back into town to show that he has been released, publicly demonstrating to the new converts the charges were false (Acts 16:40). Returning restores the honor of Lydia and the gospel message. On the other hand, in the town of Berea Paul is asked to quietly slip out of town to avoid trouble (Acts 17:14). Again, Paul complies for the sake of the gospel and the church. Two very different actions but for the same purpose: to defend the gospel.

Apostle by the Grace of God

Paul is also willing to humble himself for the sake of the churches he supported. In a letter to Christians in Corinth, Paul calls boasting foolish—and promises he isn't a fool (2 Cor 11:16)—but he boasts anyway (2 Cor 10:13-18). Paul boasts to prove he is better than some so-called apostles who were asserting their authority over the church in Corinth (2 Cor 11:5-6). Boasting strikes us as rude, but Paul is using an intentional and culturally familiar rhetorical device to subtly dig at the Corinthians. Paul insists the Corinthians seem to prefer foolishness to wisdom—so he's giving them foolishness. There is some complex cultural stuff going on here.[8] In Paul's culture, boasting was expected (as long as it was true). One boasted in one's strengths, whether on the field of battle, in the arena of games or on the rhetorical stage. And Paul had plenty to boast about. He was well-educated, had mystical experiences and worked miracles. He was far more qualified than the self-appointed Corinthian "apostles." Yet Paul behaves badly by Roman standards here because he refuses to boast in his strengths. Paul does the opposite. He boasts in his weaknesses:

> It is necessary to boast; nothing is to be gained by it, but I will go on to visions and revelations of the Lord. I know a person . . . [who] was caught up into Paradise and heard things that are not to be told, that no mortal is permitted to repeat. On behalf of such a one I will boast, but on my own behalf I will not boast, except of my weaknesses. But if I wish to boast, I will not be a fool, for I will be speaking the truth. But I refrain from it, so that no one may think better of me than what is seen in me or heard from me, even considering the exceptional character of the revelations. (2 Cor 12:1-7 NRSV)

The old "I have a friend" line is old indeed. Everyone knew Paul was talking about himself. But Paul refused to claim any advantage that would bring personal honor, even though his experience was far beyond anything the Corinthians could boast. He notes it was the truth, so he had the right to boast, but instead he boasts in his weakness. All of us today can probably name someone who boasts of their weaknesses in a passive-aggressive effort to sound self-righteous. That's not what Paul was doing. *Nobody* in ancient Rome boasted of weaknesses. Paul boasts of a weakness and an unanswered prayer. Then he adds: "I will boast all the more gladly about my weaknesses, so that Christ's power may rest on me. That is why, for Christ's sake, I delight in weaknesses, in insults, in hardships, in persecutions, in difficulties. For when I am weak, then I am strong" (2 Cor 12:9-10). That's crazy talk.

Oh, Paul is misbehaving. He is boasting about how gracious Christ is in the midst of Paul's limitations. "If I must boast, I will boast of the things that show my weakness" (2 Cor 11:30). He is boasting about the extravagant grace of God, who made Paul an apostle even though Paul didn't deserve the title. "For I am the least of the apostles and do not even deserve to be called an apostle, because I persecuted the church of God" (1 Cor 15:9).

CONCLUSION

There's no way around it. Paul thought he was special. In his defense, Christ did knock him off a horse with a blinding light and an audible word from heaven. So his feeling of grandeur, while at times irritating, was not delusional. Peter saw Christ transfigured, but Paul also saw the glorified Christ. This put Paul in an elite category.

The remarkable thing, really, is how maturely Paul handled his status. Yes, he boasted of his apostleship, but he did so defending his gospel, not his pride. It was essential that the Gentiles he ministered to trusted his pedigree, because the gospel was their only hope and he was the only person preaching it to them. Before they met Paul, the Gentiles were spiritual orphans. They were trapped in a fruitless way of life, far from

God and wandering further. Paul understood that "in Christ Jesus I became your father through the gospel" (1 Cor 4:15), and he took the role of spiritual father seriously. That's why he urged the Corinthians to "imitate me" (1 Cor 4:16). They couldn't read a Gospel; those hadn't been written yet. The only way they would see Jesus was to look at Paul. Rodney Reeves puts the matter beautifully:

> Essentially Paul was saying to his converts: "Want to know what the gospel looks like? You're looking at it. My life displays the crucifixion of Christ. I am buried with Christ through baptism. Old things have passed away in my life; everything is becoming new because the Spirit of Jesus is in me. If you follow me, you'll follow Jesus—that man you've never met but see in me." So when Paul said, "Imitate me," he wasn't being presumptuous, or controlling, or pretentious. Rather, Paul was stating the obvious: he was the only way his converts would know the gospel. They didn't have the Gospels in written form. . . . They needed someone to mentor them, to teach them, to help them live the gospel they believed. Paul was the man."[9]

Clearly, Paul was skilled rhetorically and even wrote fierce letters, but in person he was gentle with his congregations. So gentle was he, in fact, that his opponents accused him of being weak in person (2 Cor 10:10). Paul may have threatened to show up in person with fire and brimstone but instead he arrived with grace and compassion (2 Cor 10:1-2). Paul can rightly be accused of being heavy-handed with the Thessalonians, but we need to read the entire letter to understand why. Paul is also willing *not* to exercise his authority over them (1 Thess 2:7). Look at how he speaks to them:

> For our appeal does not spring from deceit or impure motives or trickery . . . , not to please mortals, but to please God . . . we never came with words of flattery or with a pretext for greed; nor did we seek praise . . . But we were gentle [a babe] among you, like a nurse tenderly caring for her own children. So deeply do we care for you . . . because you have become very dear to us. (1 Thess 2:3-8 NRSV)

In Paul's culture, he was misbehaving by not demanding pay and by describing himself as a "nursing mother." Today Paul is often critiqued for paternalism, an unattractive quality in a culture increasingly sensitive to privileged and overbearing (white) men telling everyone else how they ought to behave. Although to us, Paul may sound *paternalistic*—authoritative and bossy—his audience would have heard him as *paternal*—offering the instruction and guidance of a loving father.[10] Paul *really and truly* considered his converts his spiritual children. Just as we are overjoyed by the well-being and good decisions of our physical children, Paul was deeply affected by the decisions of his spiritual children. His frustration with Judaizers wasn't simply a theological debate. Like any good parent, Paul was angry at those he viewed as a threat to the spiritual health of his children.

The older we get, the more we see Paul's frustration with and strong language toward his colleagues and congregations as motivated by his concern that they fully understand the gospel and its implications for daily Christian living. When he asserts, "I am an apostle," he is not saying, "*I'm* important," but rather, "*What I'm saying* is important." It may be a fine distinction but it's a critical one. He is firm with his audience because what he says matters. He didn't care if they *liked* him. He needed them to *trust* him.

Bitter Medicine

Martin Luther picked up this theme in his commentary on Galatians. Paul speaks to the Galatians harshly, Luther admits. But his words are motivated by love. "A teacher chastises the pupil to reform him," Luther wrote. "The rod hurts, but correction is necessary. A father punishes his son because he loves his son. If he did not love the lad he would not punish him but let him have his own way in everything until he comes to harm. Paul beseeches the Galatians to look upon his correction as a sign that he really cared for them." Luther switches the metaphor, but continues the theme. The Galatians, and at turns the Corinthians, and all of Paul's Gentile churches, were tempted to embrace false doctrine, lose hope in God's promises, abandon the faith. This is a serious malady. "When a physician administers a bitter potion to a patient," Luther explains, "he does it to cure the patient. The fact that the medicine is bitter is no fault of the physician. The malady calls for a bitter medicine." [11]

It may rankle us when Paul claims, "I have worked much harder" than other evangelists, but we can't help but admire his determination when he continues by saying that he has also

> been in prison more frequently, been flogged more severely, and been exposed to death again and again. Five times I received from the Jews the forty lashes minus one. Three times I was beaten with rods, once I was pelted with stones, three times I was shipwrecked, I spent a night and a day in the open sea, I have been constantly on the move. I have been in danger from rivers, in danger from bandits, in

> danger from my fellow Jews, in danger from Gentiles; in danger in the city, in danger in the country, in danger at sea; and in danger from false believers. I have labored and toiled and have often gone without sleep; I have known hunger and thirst and have often gone without food; I have been cold and naked. (2 Cor 11:23-27)

Paul logged some ten thousand miles of travel for the cause of Christ, far more than just about any ancient traveler. But he doesn't boast in his accomplishments. He boasts of woes.[12] Clement, a companion of Paul's, describes the apostle as leaving behind a "notable pattern of patient endurance" (1 Clement 5:6). He may have cursed those who distorted the gospel, but he was willing to be accursed himself, if it would lead his kinsmen to Christ (Rom 9:3).

That personality of Paul's, which earned him scores of followers but few close friends, kept his eyes focused on the prize Christ set before him. Paul claimed to be special. He was. Our views on boasting might make Paul a modern jerk, but it would not have made him an ancient one. It isn't fair to judge Paul by our modern conventions on collegiality. We may not personally have enjoyed Paul's company, but when it's all said and done it's hard to deny that he left an incredible example that we are proud to follow.

two

PAUL WAS A KILLJOY

The first and greatest commandment of my (Brandon's) childhood—the rule of thumb for all Christian behavior—was a Pauline command repeated by countless revivalist preachers: "Avoid even the appearance of evil." Because of this prohibition, I could not drink root beer or ginger ale on the grounds that both of those beverages were named after alcoholic potables. They weren't alcoholic, but holding a bottle with the word "beer" on the label certainly could have had the "appearance of evil." Then there was the matter of movies. There were wholesome ones to watch at home (when we weren't boycotting Disney), but watching movies in a theater was a different issue. The people who saw you exit a movie theater late at night had no way of knowing whether you attended a G-rated movie or an R-rated one. It was safest, they argued, to avoid even the appearance of having attended an inappropriate film. And Big League Chew, the bubble gum packaged to look like chewing tobacco, was out of the question.

What Paul actually said, according to the King James Version, was that the Thessalonians should "abstain from all appearance of evil" (1 Thess 5:22). My tradition added the word "even" (*even* the appearance of evil) the same way Eve added "and you must not touch it" to God's command not to eat from the forbidden tree in the Garden of Eden (Gen 3:3). Which is to say we improved the command by making it more restrictive. Surely there is no sin in tightening things up.

I don't remember questioning whether this maxim was a verbatim quotation. It didn't matter. Everyone was confident it captured the spirit of Paul's teaching in general. Paul was our go-to guy when we needed a Bible text to stop the fun. When he wasn't urging people to avoid the appearance of evil, he was encouraging them to work hard: "Attend to your own business and work with your hands, just as we commanded you" (1 Thess 4:11 NASB). When he wasn't encouraging people to work hard, he was urging them to laugh little, to take part in "neither filthiness, nor foolish talking, nor jesting" (Eph 5:4 KJV). In short, Paul was the champion of seriousness and sobriety (Tit 2:7). What we're describing here is sometimes called the spirit of Puritanism, an impulse the American journalist H. L. Mencken once defined as "the haunting fear that someone, somewhere, may be happy."

This impulse that supposedly began with Paul made its way into American culture through New England's founding flock, the Puritans, in the eighteenth century. Puritanism, in the popular imagination, is a dour, joyless piety, with its high collars and low hems. Americans never use the term "puritanical" as a compliment. We find the same impulse across the pond in England and summarized aptly in the teaching of that most famous nineteenth-century "puritan" Charles Haddon Spurgeon:

> Christian man, remember this. Let not allowable diversions become occasions for transgression. This they will be if they

> cause waste of time; for in such a case you will be reported to your Master as a steward who has wasted his goods.[1]

The pastor urged his congregation to not misuse the talents Jesus had given them by wasting time on "diversions," even permissible ones, when they should be working. Spurgeon cautioned the Christian:

> Nor will you be blameless if your recreations weary the brain and heart, and cause a new and unrenumerative expenditure of force.[2]

In Spurgeon's reasoning, if you play too much today, you might not be able to work or pray tomorrow. To whom does the preacher turn to justify these strict instructions? To Paul, of course:

> Above all, you will be greatly censurable if there is the slightest tinge of sin about the amusement: "Abstain from all appearance of evil."[3]

There you have it. From Paul to the Puritans to a pulpit in the 1880s to my religious imagination—a heritage of sour Christianity. This is one of those problems with Paul that becomes a problem for the entire church. We can manage if Paul was generally gruff or grumpy—some people just are. But if Paul was a killjoy, and if in inspired Scripture he commanded a grim and joyless discipleship, then we begin to have problems. Plenty of people have rejected Christianity for philosophical or intellectual reasons. Anecdotally it seems to us that far more abandon the faith because they view the church as prudish. That may be right, but is Paul to blame?

Paul Policing Behaviors

It is true Paul speaks a lot about how Christ-followers should and should not behave. If we want a *list* of dos and don'ts for

Christians—what scholars call virtue and vice lists—we won't find much in the teaching of Jesus. Jesus seems to downplay the particulars of the Mosaic law in favor of more generalizing principles: love God and love your neighbor. Paul liked lists so he tells the Christians in Colossae:

> Put to death, therefore, whatever belongs to your earthly nature: sexual immorality, impurity, lust, evil desires and greed, which is idolatry. . . . You must also rid yourselves of all such things as these: anger, rage, malice, slander, and filthy language from your lips. Do not lie to each other, since you have taken off your old self with its practices. . . .
>
> Clothe yourselves with compassion, kindness, humility, gentleness and patience. Bear with each other and forgive one another. (Col 3:5-13)

Paul is using a clothing metaphor. Christians should take off vices as we do dirty, old clothes. Then we should put on virtues as we do clean clothes. We certainly don't dispute any of the vices or virtues, but we can't help but point out that Paul lists twice as many don'ts as dos.[4] This doesn't settle well with a generation that believes Christians should be known for what we are *for* rather than what we are *against.*

Paul has similarly restrictive instructions for other congregations. One might assume there is too much horsing around going on in Ephesus for Paul's taste. There Paul denounces obscene speech, and rightly so in our opinion. But Paul also doesn't care for silliness: "Entirely out of place is obscene, silly, and vulgar talk" (Eph 5:4 NRSV). Should "silly" be placed in the same list as "obscene" and "vulgar"? Paul appears to think so and our spiritual mentors certainly took this to heart. Horsing around in the back of the church van was denounced with the same gravity as other serious vices. Giggling could well lead to fornicating; after all, Paul lists silliness and fornication in the same sentence (Eph 5:3-4).

There were other problems in Ephesus. There were some women in the church there who didn't have jobs. Some women in first-century Roman culture ran businesses and held responsibilities outside the home. More often women worked in the home, running the household and raising children. (We'll get into how Paul treats women in chapter five.) These women in Ephesus appear to be wealthy widows, younger and apparently without children, which is to say that they weren't employed outside the home but they also didn't have duties inside the home. It's likely they were sponsoring their own house church and visiting other ones in their copious free time. Paul doesn't approve of their activities because with all that free time "they learn to be idle, gadding about from house to house; and they are not merely idle, but also gossips and busybodies, saying what they should not say" (1 Tim 5:13 NRSV). In Paul's mind, their leisure is getting them into trouble, so his solution is for them to get to work: "So I would have younger widows marry, bear children, and manage their households, so as to give the adversary no occasion to revile us" (1 Tim 5:14).

Paul certainly didn't have any problem telling people how they ought to behave.

Keeping up Appearances

Paul's commands to the women of Ephesus raise another concern of his: *appearances*. Paul was adamant that Christians should live a holy life. But avoiding the appearance of evil has less to do with holiness and more to do with other people's perception of our holiness. Jesus urged us to do our good deeds out of sight and "not to practice your righteousness in front of others to be seen by them" (Mt 6:1). By contrast, Paul wanted his disciples to act righteously in plain sight of their neighbors.

For example, Paul encourages the Christians in Thessalonica to "live in a way that pleases God" (1 Thess 4:1 NLT). One of the ways to please God is to "lead a quiet life," which is to say, "mind your own business and work with your hands" (1 Thess 4:11). They are instructed to do this not only because it pleases God, but also so that their "daily life may win the respect of outsiders" (1 Thess 4:12).

The same principle is at work in another passage and for another congregation. Paul instructs the young pastor Titus to "encourage the young men" in his congregation "to be self-controlled" (Tit 2:6) and Titus should be the example. Titus is encouraged to show "integrity, seriousness and soundness of speech" in his teaching. Here again Paul clarifies the reason for this conduct: "so that those who oppose you may be ashamed because they have nothing bad to say about us" (Tit 2:8). Paul even makes public perception a requirement for clergy. Deacons, he writes in 1 Tim 3:7, should "have a good reputation with outsiders."

The Battle for Respectability

American Christians will often say that true character is what you do when no one is watching. It's easy to put on a show, but what really matters is what we believe and how we behave in private. In stark contrast to this perspective, Paul was very concerned about how his followers' behavior was perceived by others. The reason for this, to be frank, is because the reputation of some of Paul's churches was in the sewer.

The Roman Empire in Paul's day was awash in new religions. Some of them were known for outrageous behavior. Bacchus (also known as Dionysus), the Roman god of wine, freedom and intoxication (ecstasy), was honored by festival meals called *Bacchanalia.* A Roman historian named Livy, who lived a generation before Christ, described the bacchanalia in these terms:

> From the time that the rites were performed in common, men mingling with women and the freedom of darkness added, no form of crime, no sort of wrongdoing, was left untried. There were more lustful practices among men with one another than among women. . . . To consider nothing wrong . . . was the highest form of religious devotion among them.[5]

Because immorality was a common feature of new religions popping up in Rome, Romans were probably predisposed to believe the rumors circulating about those new followers of the Way. Within a century of the resurrection, Christians were accused of all manner of misbehavior. Around 177, the Christian philosopher Athenagoras wrote an open letter to defend Christians, in which he identified three common charges:

> Three things are alleged against us: atheism, Thyestean feasts [cannibalism], Oedipodean intercourse [incest]. But if these charges are true, spare no class: proceed at once against our crimes; destroy us root and branch, with our wives and children, if any Christian is found to live like the brutes. And yet even the brutes do not touch the flesh of their own kind.[6]

Athenagoras insists these are only "idle tales and empty slanders."[7] Even so, the fact that such charges were floating around out there is evidence that Paul wasn't being paranoid when he urged his fellow believers to consider how their behavior would be interpreted by watching skeptical neighbors.

Ancient News Flash: Christians Kill and Eat Babies!

Around 200 AD, the Church father Tertullian complained, "We are said to be the most criminal of men, on the score of our sacramental baby-killing, and the baby-eating that goes with it and the incest that follows the banquet."[8] How can the Christians be guilty of incest if even "the brutes" won't commit that crime? It is likely that confusion about drinking baby's blood stemmed from the fact that Christians drank the "blood" of Christ and ate his "body" in the ritual of Communion. It's possible that rumors of incest spread when Christian men and women who referred to each other as "brothers" and "sisters" (in Christ) eventually married.

Roman pagans were not the church's only critics. Fairly quickly Paul earned a reputation among the Jewish community for teaching Jews to ignore the law of Moses and abandon the age-old traditions. The Hebrew Scriptures were clear that circumcision was the act God ordained as a sign of his covenant with his people—an eternal sign. Abraham was commanded to circumcise every male, even Gentiles that came into his household, "Whether born in your household or bought with your money, they must be circumcised. My covenant in your flesh is to be an everlasting covenant" (Gen 17:13). Paul insisted that a Gentile could enjoy a covenant with God without being circumcised. Many Jews in Jerusalem were left wondering, if Paul was willing to reject circumcision what other part of the law would he dispense with? One of the (many) times Paul was arrested, it was on the charge that he was an open enemy of Judaism: "This is the man who teaches everyone everywhere against our people and our law and this place" (Acts 21:28). Some Jews considered Paul such a threat to the people of Israel, that they hatched a plot to have him killed (Acts 23:12).

As if dealing with Roman pagans and Jewish opponents was not enough, even some Christians misunderstood the message Paul preached about salvation through faith in Christ apart from the law. Some Christians apparently had the same impression as Paul's Jewish critics, and believed that salvation by faith—a law-free gospel—meant they could do whatever they wanted. Like the revelers of Bacchus for whom considering nothing wrong was "the highest form of devotion," they thought being free from the law of Moses meant being free from any moral code whatsoever. Since there is no condemnation for those in Christ (Rom 8:1), if one sins, grace covers it. This led some to conclude that the more they sinned, the more grace they received (Rom 6:1). What a deal! Jude knew some so-called Christians like this. He writes about false teachers who "have wormed their way into your churches, saying that God's marvelous grace allows us to live immoral lives" (Jude 4 NLT). No doubt some of those false teachers claimed Paul for their inspiration.

The problem for Paul was that not all the slander was baseless. Some of the rumors were indeed true. Paul had indeed preached a law-free gospel in Corinth. They took it to heart. But they misunderstood it and kept living the same way as they lived before they believed. A common custom among the wealthier folks in Corinth were dinners called *convivia*.

> A *convivium* was usually a smaller private dinner party. . . . In many ways the most important slave at a *convivium* was the wineserver. He was expected to be young and sexually

> attractive, catering to pederastic [homosexual] lust. . . . The Roman *convivium* was legendary for fostering a degree of decadence of the "palate" as well as the "pillow."[9]

The *convivium* concluded with the *symposion,* a drinking fest. Women who attended were viewed as prostitutes. In addition to drunkenness and sexual immorality, the meat served at these feasts was typically offered to a god or goddess (1 Cor 8). Elite guests ate choice meats first while poorer guests waited for whatever was left (1 Cor 11:21). These dinner parties were known for the very kind of misbehaving that Paul condemns among the Corinthians. Paul may have been summing up these parties when he commanded the Corinthians

> But now I am writing to you that you must not associate with anyone who claims to be a brother or sister but is sexually immoral or greedy, an idolater or slanderer, a drunkard or swindler. Do not even eat with such people. (1 Cor 5:11)

Some Christians in Corinth appear to have believed the gospel gave them license to sin. In 1 Corinthians 5, Paul denounces an especially disturbing instance of sexual immorality "of a kind that even pagans do not tolerate." Someone in the Corinthian congregation was sleeping with his stepmother. And instead of grieving and disciplining the man, the church was proud! (1 Cor 5:2). Proud of what? Proud that by the grace of Christ, they were free to do whatever they pleased.

The majority of Christians didn't deserve it, but the earliest Christian community had earned a reputation as a bunch of immoral people who flouted the law of God and behaved worse than the pagans—and that's saying something. It's little wonder that Paul was quick to command the churches to live lives that brought honor, instead of shame, on the gospel of Christ. Paul never sugarcoated the gospel. He knew it was foolishness to the Gentiles and a stumbling block to the Jews. There was no need to add to the offense of the gospel by behaving badly. If people were going to assume the worst, Christians needed to be especially diligent to not add truth to the slander. They needed to behave so nobly, to wear their righteousness so obviously, that "those who oppose [them] may be ashamed because they have nothing bad to say about [them]" (Tit 2:8).

So, Can We Have Fun or Not?

We're sort of back where we began. Paul may have had good reason to encourage his converts to behave themselves. But that doesn't solve the problem. It's hard to shake the feeling that Paul advocated a different sort of discipleship than Jesus advocated. Jesus had a sense of humor. His comment "you are worth more than many sparrows" was tongue in cheek (Mt 10:31). *The Message* paraphrase catches the spirit of Jesus' comment: "You're worth more than a million canaries." Jesus could laugh. Paul was serious.

Where Paul regularly introduced new religious regulations for his converts, Jesus regularly relieved his disciples of the harsh tradition of religious dos and don'ts. On the face of it this appears to be an open contradiction. But it isn't. It's a matter of context. It's a matter of different groups of disciples facing different problems. Jesus preached to religious insiders, groups of humble farmers wearied with rules and boundaries. "When he saw the crowds," the Gospels tell us, "he had compassion on them, because they were harassed and helpless, like sheep without a shepherd" (Mt 9:36). The law was often referred to as a "yoke," for it kept adherents lined up and working as a yoke did for oxen. In fact, deciding to leave Judaism was often termed "casting off the yoke" of the law. Jesus looked at his wearied countrymen and said, "Come to me, all you who are weary and burdened, and I will give you rest. Take *my* yoke upon you and learn from me, for I am gentle and humble in heart, and you will find rest for your souls. For *my* yoke is easy and my burden is light" (Mt 11:28-30, emphasis added).

Jesus' hearers knew what he meant. He was offering an easier yoke than the law. His hearers were not living riotously. Generally, they were trying to behave as they should, but every aspect of their lives was regulated. The people's foreign oppressors were keeping them so poor that they lived their lives at mere subsistence level. Already there was little room for joy in living; then along came the religious elite heaping on more rules about seeming minutiae. "And you experts in the law, woe to you, because you load people down with burdens they can hardly carry, and you yourselves will not lift one finger to help them" (Lk 11:46). To people in this situation, Jesus offered comfort.

Paul faced disciples with a very different set of challenges. Some of them were from a privileged class, and instead of finding comfort in the gospel they distorted it to placate their consciences. Paul was introducing a minimum moral standard to a group of immoral converts ignorant of God's law as it was communicated in Israel's Scriptures. Ultimately Paul was offering his readers liberty, but the kind of liberty that comes from submitting to a new master. The Gentiles, before following Jesus, were slaves to sin (Rom 6:6). If they continue to sin, they remain slaves to sin (Rom 6:16). Paul is telling them to follow Christ and find freedom. He's telling them that to find their lives, they first have to lose them. That's Jesus' message too (Mt 10:39).

The truth is, Paul himself modulated his instructions for different audiences, as local needs dictated. The Christians in Galatia were being oppressed by rigid Jewish-background believers who claimed that pagan converts had to keep the law of Moses to please God. To these Christians Paul gives a very un-Pauline-sounding exhortation: "It is for freedom that Christ has set us free. Stand firm, then, and do not let yourselves be burdened again by a yoke of slavery" (Gal 5:1). Don't bind yourself to the law of Moses; enjoy the liberty of Christ. Here and elsewhere, Paul was reading his audience and giving the encouragement or corrective each context called for. I was told many times as a child that this was the job of the preacher: to comfort the afflicted and afflict the comfortable.

In the age of social media, when all our private moments can be made public, speaking truth in context is a very difficult thing to do. A sermon preached to a group of new believers that needs to be comforted by the gracious forgiveness of Christ can be broadcast worldwide in an instant, where it can be viewed by self-righteous religious types (like ourselves) who need to be challenged by the righteous demands of Christ.

Fullness of Joy

Paul was concerned about the reputation of the gospel. The behavior of some in his flock was bringing disrepute upon the message, and he knew that how Christians live will influence how people perceive the validity of the gospel message. This was not a new idea. God wanted Israel to live wisely to win the Gentiles (Mic 4:2). Jesus called his disciples "the light of the world" that would draw the nations to salvation. It is in this spirit that Paul urges his fellow believers to live "so that your daily life may win the respect of outsiders" (1 Thess 4:12).

Context is critical. Jesus was dealing with self-righteous Pharisees who wanted to be admired for their piety. The solution? As disciples we should do our good deeds in secret (Mt 6). Paul was dealing with a church slandered as cannibals, accused of gross immorality, reveling in misbehaviors. The solution? We disciples should do our good deeds in sight, letting our neighbors see our godly lives so that the rumors are proven false. Even though this behavior can easily become distorted and result in image management, or pharisaism, that's not what Paul was advocating.

Keeping on the straight and narrow is often about staying out of the ditches *on either side* of the path. If we illustrate the Christian life as a road, a *Way* (as the first Christians called it), then we note there is a ditch on each side. In this matter, on the left side we might see the danger of being a poor example to the world. To stay out of this ditch, we would do well to live in ways that show the transforming power of the gospel. We should let our light shine.

But there is still a ditch on the other side: hedge building. Ancient Jews encouraged keeping the law—as they should. A *khumra* is a requirement that exceeds the actual law; it is a precaution. Traditionally, the practice came from Deuteronomy 22:8 where we are told to put a fence around our roofs when we build a house to prevent someone from falling off. The idea is to put in place rules that protect us from transgressing the law. There is some wisdom here. Proverbs wisely instructs young men to stay away from the streets where the prostitutes live (Prov 7:25). Likewise, if we are to keep the sabbath holy we should do not work on the sabbath. To avoid this danger, all manner of rules were created to help someone avoid the risk of work and thus breaking sabbath: You can only walk so far on the sabbath. Mothers couldn't cook a hot meal on the sabbath because lighting a fire might be work. But now we have fallen into the ditch. Like the Pharisees, we insist there should be no healings on the sabbath. We have protected our reputation in the community, but now Jesus is looking us in the eye and asking, "Is it lawful to heal on the Sabbath?" (Mt 12:10). We find ourselves telling our youth not to drink ginger ale to avoid any appearance of evil.

But of course we bring our own baggage to our interpretation of Paul. Return with us to Paul's words in 1 Thessalonians 5:22 used by our spiritual mentors to kill our joy: "Avoid even the appearance of evil." When the King James Version of the Bible was translated, this old English idiom "abstain from all appearance of evil" connoted that one should "avoid evil, no matter what form it appears in." This sense is evident in newer English translations. For example, the NIV renders the phrase, "reject every kind of evil." That's a very helpful modern translation, but those of us grew up with the older translations and interpretations have a hard time shaking the feeling that Paul is always looking over our shoulder ready to disapprove of our good times.

Paul was admittedly a serious sort. (Frequent beatings and persecution will likely have that effect.) If he were around today, he may not be the life of the party. But when we review his statements about the seriousness of the life of faith, let us place on the other side of the scale his constant reminders that Christian life should be characterized, above all, by joy. Paul talks about joy more than twenty times in his letters. Joy is a fruit of the Spirit and a fundamental characteristic of God; every Christian should exude joyfulness (Gal 5:22). Paul frequently prayed that his friends would lead lives of obedience, yes, but *joyful* obedience (Phil 1:25). In all this, Paul urged Christians to embrace a tension that remains difficult to maintain today, that is, recognizing that full joy comes from living within the guardrails of God's commands.

three

PAUL WAS A RACIST

Martin Luther, the great German scholar-monk who sparked the Protestant Reformation, had a complex view of Jews and Judaism. Early in his career, he protected them and honored them as the ethnic family members of Abraham and Jesus. Later in life, though, he had a dramatic (and disgusting) change of heart. After years of watching German Jews fail to accept the gospel of Christ, Luther announced, "I do not wish to have anything more to do with any Jew."

Luther wrote this in a book called *On the Jews and Their Lies* (1543). The title of the piece tells you what you need to know about its tone. In part eleven, the most infamous section of the book, Luther answers the practical question "What shall we Christians do with this rejected and condemned people, the Jews?" and crosses the line from cranky ranting into racist-Uncle-Marty hate speech. Since Christians apparently cannot convert the Jews, Luther advises, "First, to set fire to their synagogues or schools and to bury and cover with dirt whatever will not burn." Here he appeals to Moses (Deut 13:12-18) for support. "Second," Luther continues, "I advise that their houses also be razed and destroyed." Their prayer books and Talmudic writings should be confiscated and their rabbis forbidden to teach "on pain of life and limb." Again Luther cites Moses, using against the Jews with intentional irony the law they revere. Here's the line that makes our stomachs turn: "I recommend putting a flail, an ax, a hoe, a spade, a distaff, or a spindle into the hands of young, strong Jews and Jewesses and letting them earn their bread in the sweat of their brow." This line of thought inspired the enterprising young Adolf Hitler to do essentially that, consigning Jews of Europe to "work" in concentration camps. Hitler shared with Luther the deep desire to "be rid of the unbearable, devilish burden of the Jews"—unfortunately, Luther's words, not Hitler's. We may find some solace in the fact that Luther didn't quote Paul when he advised burning down the homes and synagogues of German Jews. But he clearly believed the apostle was on his side. "As St. Paul says," Luther reasoned, "they are consigned to wrath; the more one tries to help them the baser and more stubborn they become. Leave them to their own devices."[1]

After the horrors of the Holocaust and in light of ongoing racial tensions in the United States, we cannot consign racism in general or anti-Semitism specifically to the status of a personality quirk. If Paul was an anti-Semite, that creates a serious problem for Christianity. Maybe a terminal one. We could handle a cranky and unpleasant Paul on a personal level without affecting our faith too much. He can have his moments, like we all do, without compromising the integrity of the gospel. But if he hated a race of people—condemned them to torture and death on the basis of ethnicity—then we have found a flaw in Paul we can't sweep under the rug.

Before we go too far, we should take a moment to define the terms we'll use in this discussion. Conversations about race and racism are complicated for many reasons, but among them is the vocabulary we employ. Twenty-first-century Americans talk about individual racism, systemic racism and cultural racism. We can further subdivide these categories, for example, by discussing the difference between overt and inferential racism or identifying microaggressions. For the sake of the present conversation, when we say "racism" we mean the belief that some races or ethnicities are superior to others. A comment is racist, whether it is complimentary or derogatory, if it is made about someone and attributed to them because of their race. The fact is, no matter how we define terms, we'll be working with concepts entirely foreign to Paul and his first-century audience. What we really want to know—what is essential for us to know—is, was Paul a racist by our twenty-first-century standards?

Lazy Cretans, Stupid Galatians and Jewish Dogs

The charge of racism against Paul is based on a number of strong statements the apostle makes against members of non-Jewish ethnic groups, statements we, by modern standards, would consider politically incorrect, if not outright racist. The charge of anti-Semitism arises from a more systematic representation of Jews in Paul's writings as violent, dishonest and adversarial. Paul went first to the Jews, then to the Gentiles. We're going to go the other way around, discussing first Paul's comments about Gentiles.

In a letter to Titus, a young pastor in Crete, Paul urges Titus to "rebuke" his congregation "sharply" (Tit 1:13). They are intractable people, Paul claims. "One of Crete's own prophets has said it: 'Cretans are always liars, evil brutes, lazy gluttons'" (Tit 1:12). Paul here quotes the Cretan poet Epimenides[2] and he doesn't refute the claim. Instead he affirms it: "This saying is true" (1:13). Perhaps Paul didn't invent new ways to dress down the Gentiles. But he wasn't afraid to use an existing slur when it suited his purposes.

In his letter to the Christians in Galatia, Paul refers to them with what feels like another slur: "foolish Galatians" (Gal 3:1). The Romans named that entire region of central Turkey by the generic title Galatia, a Roman mispronunciation of the word *Celtic*. In the previous centuries, Celts had migrated into the northern section of central Turkey. (Those Celts show up everywhere!) They kept to themselves and didn't integrate into the Greek empire. Since they didn't speak Greek, the Greeks considered them "barbarians." Greeks thought all foreign languages sounded like "bar-bar" (the Greek equivalent of "blah-blah"), so the term "barbarian" essentially meant someone who didn't speak Greek.

Later, in the Roman era, strong negative stereotypes attached to the Galatians. They were widely caricatured as being "large, unpredictable simpletons, ferocious and highly dangerous when angry, but without stamina and easy to trick."[3] Basically your standard oaf. By Paul's lifetime, other peoples, including a large number of (Greek-speaking) Jews, had migrated into the southern region of Galatia. They referred to themselves by the names of the Roman provinces in which they lived. It really wasn't polite to lump them with those Galatian barbarians in the north. They were civilized, after all. Thus, Luke is careful to call them by their preferred names, such as Lycaonians (Acts 14:11) or people from "Cappadocia, Pontus and Asia, Phrygia and Pamphylia" (Acts 2:9-10). When Paul calls the church a bunch of "foolish Galatians," it would be a lot like calling people from the South (our home region) "rednecks," "hillbillies" or "white trash." Paul does this on purpose. One scholar has noted, "it is part of Paul's reproach that he equates them with the barbarous people who had given their name to the province, and who themselves had a quite independent reputation for simple-mindedness."[4]

Colorful as Paul could be in his interactions with Gentiles, Paul reserves his harshest language for his fellow countrymen, the Jews. He calls them Christ-killers who have their hearts set against the things of God. Not only have they "killed the Lord Jesus" but also "the prophets," who were proclaiming God's word, and most recently they "also drove us out. They displease God and are hostile to everyone" (1 Thess 2:15). In this way, Paul writes, "they always heap up their sins to the limit" (1 Thess 2:16). He quotes selectively from the prophet Isaiah to suggest that this resistance to God's work is Israel's *modus operandi*. Quoting Isaiah 65:2, Paul claims Israel is a "disobedient and obstinate people" (Rom 10:21). Israel's obstinacy isn't theoretical for Paul. "Five times I received from the Jews the forty lashes minus one," for preaching the gospel of Christ (2 Cor 11:24). At his most virulent he even calls some Jews "dogs, those evildoers, those mutilators of the flesh" and "enemies of the cross of Christ" whose "destiny is destruction, their god is their stomach, and their glory is in their shame" because their "mind is set on earthly things" (Phil 3:2, 18, 19). By comparison, Paul's characterization of Cretans as lazy and Galatians as simple-minded is almost complimentary.

If we are tempted to dismiss Paul's comments about lazy Cretans and foolish Galatians as rhetorical flourish, we have to admit that these charges against Jews feel more personal and more powerfully charged. And yet here again, as we've seen other places, Paul's point of view is complex. Paul argues consistently and persistently that there is no difference between Jews and Gentiles in God's eyes, as we shall see below. He nevertheless repeatedly insists that the Israelites reserve a special role in God's plan of salvation. He poses an important rhetorical question to the Romans: "What advantage, then, is there in being a Jew, or what value is there in circumcision?" (Rom 3:1). It's tempting to assume that the answer is, "None at all." That would seem consistent with Paul's teaching elsewhere. But Paul surprises both us and the Romans. What advantage is there in being a Jew? "Much in every way! First of all, the Jews have been entrusted with the very words of God" (Rom 3:2). The law of Moses was God's gift to humanity. And he gave it to his people, Israel, to steward it and share it with others. That's why Paul says over and over in Romans that God's salvation is extended "first to the Jew, then to the Gentile" (Rom 1:16; see also Rom 2:9-10). The gift God extended to his people, they can now extend to all the peoples of the earth.

Who Were the "Jews"?

Paul will seem bafflingly inconsistent in his opinions about Jews until we recognize how he's using this key term in his writings. Most modern people use the term *Jew* to refer to someone who is Jewish religiously (someone who adheres to Judaism) or to a person of Jewish ancestry, whether that person is of Middle Eastern or European descent. For most Westerners *Jew* is an umbrella term that includes an entire race *or* religion. Even the biblical terms *Jew, Israelite* and *Hebrew* are to us all different ways to say the *same* thing. That's why when Paul charges "the Jews" with the death of Jesus, we hear him saying that the entire Jewish race and/or religion is somehow responsible for the death of Christ. This is classic anti-Semitic rhetoric. It is also *not* what Paul meant.

When Paul chastises Jews, he singles out specific parties within what we today would call first-century Judaism. The first group he rails against is the Judaizers. Galatians 2:14 is the only time he identifies them by name. There the word *Judaize* is a verb, and only Young's Literal Translation renders it that way: "If thou, being a Jew, in the manner of the nations dost live, and not in the manner of the Jews, how the nations dost thou compel to Judaize?" Most other translations translate this strange term, "to Judaize," as a phrase: "You are a Jew, yet you live like a Gentile and not like a Jew. How is it, then, that you force Gentiles to follow Jewish customs?" (NIV). The term *Judaizer* is shorthand for Jewish-background Christians who believe that pagan converts to Christianity have to keep the law of Moses, and in particular to be circumcised, in order truly to be "in." Elsewhere Paul refers to these people who themselves profess faith in Christ as "the circumcision group" (Gal 2:12) and "the circumcision" (Eph 2:11). When he's really worked up, he refers to them as "dogs, those evildoers, those mutilators of the flesh" (Phil 3:2). Paul is not calling *all* Jews these things. Rather, he is referring to a small group of ethnic Israelites who are followers of Jesus but are distorting the gospel by teaching that Gentile converts must behave like ethnic Israelites if they want to be saved.

From here, things get tricky. In our English translations the word "Jew" shows up a lot in the words of Paul. Even in Galatians 2:14, which we just said doesn't apply to all Jews, Paul uses the word several times. This time, the problem isn't with Paul but with our translations. The word most often translated "Jew" (*Ioudaios*) can also be translated "Judean." In fact, it is probably *better* translated "Judean."[5] For many centuries, scholars and translators have treated the terms "Judean" and "Jew" as if they were interchangeable, but the fact is how the word should be translated depends on who is using it. Outsiders—Romans at the time of Christ and biblical scholars since then—have used the terms *Jew* and *Judean* interchangeably to apply to all people either of Israelite ancestry or adherence to Judaism. Insiders—Israelites at the time of Christ—used the term *Judean* to describe a specific subset of people within Judaism.

This is not surprising. It's how ethnic identity works. Outsiders tend to lump together people who are different from them. Insiders tend to make clear distinctions among themselves. "Jewish" insiders in Jesus' day (and Paul's) tended to self-identify based on their family and their provenance. Thus Jesus was known as the son of Joseph (Lk 3:23; Jn 1:45; 6:42) or "the carpenter's son" (Mt 13:55). He was also identified by geography, where he was from, when called Jesus of "Nazareth in Galilee" (Mt 21:11), or "Jesus of Galilee" (Mt 26:69), or "Jesus of Nazareth" (i.e., Mt 26:71; Mk 10:47; Lk 18:37; Jn 18:5). Though Jesus is identified a number of ways, he is *never* identified as an *Ioudaios* (Jew/Judean) except by outsiders. The magi who travel from the east to visit the boy Jesus come looking for "the king of the Jews/Judeans" (Mt 2:2). The Samaritan woman with whom Jesus spoke at a well thought he was a Judean (Jn 4). The Romans who executed Jesus put a sign over his head that read, "King of the Judeans" (or "King of the Jews") (Mt 27:37; Mk 15:26; Lk 23:38; Jn 19:19). None of his countrymen called him that. Instead, they identified him as "king of Israel" (Jn 1:49; 12:13).

The reason no Israelite ever called Jesus an *Ioudaios* (Judean) is simple: he wasn't one. Israelites referred to themselves collectively as "Israelites." Among themselves, they specified. Jesus was a Galilean. Herod was an Idumean. Judas was a Judean. When Paul described himself, he said, "I am an Israelite myself, a descendant of Abraham, from the tribe of Benjamin" (Rom 11:1). Luke, who was writing to a Roman audience, glosses over this insider distinction and uses a term his Roman audience will understand. When Paul is arrested by Roman soldiers in Jerusalem, Luke cites Paul as saying, "I am a Jew, from Tarsus in Cilicia" (Acts 21:39). But Paul calls himself an *Ioudaios* (Jew/Judean) only once in his letters and that was when lumping himself into one of two categories, Jews and Gentiles (Gal 2:15). Luke isn't misquoting Paul. He is glossing over a fine distinction that would have been lost on his Roman readers, a distinction that would likely have only confused them.

Outsiders tended to lump all Israelites together as Judeans ("Jews"), but we do something similar today. If we are traveling in England and someone asked if we are "Yankees," we would answer, "Yes," because in England the term *Yankee* refers to someone from the United States. However, if we are traveling in Michigan and someone asked us if we are "Yankees," we would say, "Absolutely not." Because in Michigan the term *Yankee* refers to someone from the Northern United States (and these southern boys retain their regional pride). We're not lying to our British friends. It's a fine distinction that would be lost on most of them.

Our subject, though, is not how Luke describes Paul to Romans. The issue is how Paul uses the term *Jew*. When Paul derides "the Jews" for killing Jesus and for persecuting him for preaching the gospel, he is referring to a specific group of people, Judeans. "Judean," the way Paul and most of his countrymen at the time used the word, had ethnic, geographic and religious connotations. To be Judean meant, at the most basic level, to be from Judea (ethnic and geographic). Paul himself was Judean in this broad sense, because he was raised in Jerusalem. Just as important as geography, to be Judean meant that your particular religious devotion was centered on the temple of Yahweh in Jerusalem. Compare this to the Samaritans who also were

Israelites but who identified the temple on Mt. Gerazim as the true temple of Yahweh. Inscriptions on a building on the island of Delos mention "the Israelites on Delos who make first-fruit offerings to the temple on Mt. Gerizim."[6] In other words, when Paul charges the *Ioudaioi* with killing Jesus and the prophets, with opposing his ministry and putting roadblocks in front of Gentile converts, he's not implicating all "Jews." He's condemning "the Judeans." And he's absolutely right.

More specifically, it is unlikely Paul was referring to every Israelite living in Judea. He really wasn't thinking of the olive farmer in Bethphage or the persimmon grower in Hyrcania. Paul had in mind the Judeans who were ardently defending the temple and their homeland against Romans and anyone else who threatened it.

Defend our Temple!

In AD 40, Caesar Gaius attempted to have his statue erected in the temple in Jerusalem. Judeans were ready to fight Rome to stop it, but Gaius died before he could finish the project. Tensions were mounting again during Paul's ministry. (They erupted in AD 66, about the time Paul died.) During Paul's ministry, Judeans were calling upon their countrymen to return to the homeland to defend it (and the temple). It's no coincidence that Jesus, Stephen and Paul were all charged with the same crime: preaching against the temple (in Judea) and threatening to destroy it.

When Paul writes to Jewish audiences and uses the word *Ioudaioi*, these are the Judeans he had in mind. But when Paul writes to Gentile Christians in Galatia and says in Galatians 3:28, for example, "There is neither Jew nor Gentile, neither slave nor free, nor is there male and female, for you are all one in Christ Jesus," he is probably using *Ioudaioi* in the way Gentiles would have understood it (meaning "all Israelites") by contrasting Jews with Gentiles (the two groups that really didn't like each other). In either case, both his Jewish and Gentile audiences would have understood completely Paul's point.

Was Paul an Ancient Racist?

By our modern standards of racism, there were plenty of racists in antiquity and plenty of anti-Semites. The Greek poet Petronius ridiculed the Jews and their religious convictions by pointing out what he considered the nitpicking nature of their piety:

> The Jew may worship his pig-god and clamour in the ears of high heaven, but unless he also cuts back with the knife the region of his groin, and unless he unlooses by art the knotted head, he shall go forth from the holy city cast forth from the people, and transgress the sabbath by breaking the law of fasting.[7]

While modern racism is often associated with skin color, ancients rarely commented on such things. They certainly noted that Africans were dark skinned, but generally they admired Africans as fierce warriors.[8] Instead of being based on skin color, racism in the ancient world was more often based on religion, ethnicity and geography. And these categories were profoundly interrelated, almost inseparable. Thus when ancients talked about a "Judean," they were referring to someone who lived in Judea, but they *also* meant someone of a certain ethnicity (Judean), *and* they meant someone of a particular religious persuasion who worshiped at the Yahweh temple in Judea (Jerusalem).

There's no denying Paul employed slurs and dealt in stereotypes that most Americans today, Christian or otherwise, would consider racist. In our stumbling journey toward racial equality in the United States, we have essentially outlawed certain words. Changing the nation's vocabulary hasn't necessarily changed the nation's heart, but it's an important first step. We are both grateful for the progress. As the adoptive father of two children who are both ethnically different from me, I (Brandon) am grateful that the kind of overtly racist, hateful language I grew up hearing frequently is much less common today. In a way I never would have imagined possible, I now take racially insensitive language *personally.*

I (Randy) can relate but for very different reasons. Even though *bulé* is a derogatory term for "white-skins," I didn't mind being called a *bulé* while we lived in Indonesia because it had no emotional baggage for me. When I preached in villages, sometimes in a sermon I would refer to myself as the *bulé* pastor for the chuckles it caused. That all changed one day when my wife and I were in town with our two young boys and some kids started calling them *bulé.* Suddenly it mattered. Some poor Indonesian boys got a dose of righteous indignation in the form of a tongue-lashing from me. Words have power. The old American proverb about sticks and stones is absolutely wrong. We taught it to our children as "Sticks and stones may break my bones, but words cut even deeper." This, we think, is a more biblical understanding of the weight of words. James understood the power of speech to bless or to curse (Jas 3:5-12).

It is critical to understand that Paul uses slurs and stereotypes against the Galatians and Cretans for rhetorical effort. That was, in first-century Rome, a perfectly acceptable thing to do. So when Paul calls the Galatians "foolish Galatians," he is not accepting the stereotype. Rather, he is trying to rattle them by implying that in this instance they are validating the stereotype. Yes, he refuses to call them by their preferred ethnic self-designation (Pamphylians or Lycaonians). When my (Randy's) wife calls me an idiot, it doesn't have the sting of an insult where we live. It rattles me and causes me to wonder what I did wrong. But someone from another region who didn't know us might assume she was insulting me. Likewise, if we don't know Paul's relationship with the Galatians, we can assume he is insulting them. But his history with them says otherwise. He was stoned—literally pelted with rocks until presumed dead—by these people (Acts 14:19). Even so, Paul visited this region at least four times. In fact, immediately after being stoned, he revisited the region's churches because he was concerned for the fledgling mission there and battles the so-called pillars of the church on their behalf. These are not the actions of someone who despised Galatians. They could not doubt his deep love and commitment to them.

The same is true, of course, when we consider Paul's words about the Cretans. Cretans were called liars because they denied that Zeus was immortal. They were ridiculed by their own prophets for not understanding religious truths. Paul was repeating this proverb to Titus whose job was to explain the truth of the gospel to them, with the hope that their capacity for religious studies had expanded since Epimenides's indictment. Paul intended this letter to be read not only by Titus but by Titus *in front of the congregations.*[9] Paul knew the Cretans would hear this statement. It wasn't a whispered comment to Titus. It was a jab at the Cretan Christians to stop acting like Cretan pagans. Furthermore, Paul has left one of his best workers in Crete. He has not abandoned them. He has invested in them. He traveled repeatedly to the area. These are not the actions of someone who hates Cretans or who is hated by them. In fact, Paul tells Titus, "Greet those [Cretans] who love us in the faith" (Tit 3:15). Paul speaks kindly to them and not down at them, even adopting the negative ethnic stereotype for himself:

> Remind them to be subject to rulers and authorities, to be obedient, to be ready for every good work, to speak evil of no one, to avoid quarreling, to be gentle, and to show every courtesy to everyone. For *we ourselves* were once foolish, disobedient, led astray, slaves to various passions and pleasures, passing our days in malice and envy, despicable, hating one another. (Tit 3:1-3 NRSV, emphasis added)

Note Paul's inclusive language, "*We ourselves* were once foolish."

But what about those Jewish "dogs"? Surely this one was a racist comment. Sometimes Paul blasts the Jews, while elsewhere he expresses a profound sense of pride about his Jewish background. He brags he comes from a family of faithful Jews, "I thank God, whom I serve, *as my ancestors did* . . ." (2 Tim 1:3, emphasis added). He is quick to associate with the Israelites. "I myself am an Israelite, a descendant of Abraham, a member of the tribe of Benjamin" (Rom 11:1 NRSV). Not only is Paul willing to claim his Jewishness, he goes a step further and insists that he personally was a really good Jew. He was "circumcised on the eighth day, of the people of Israel, of the tribe of Benjamin, a Hebrew of Hebrews; in regard to the law, a Pharisee; as for zeal, persecuting the church; as for righteousness based on the law, faultless" (Phil 3:5-6). When anyone questions his faithfulness to the God of Israel, he quickly asserts his religious credentials. "I am a Jew, born in Tarsus of Cilicia, but brought up in this city," Paul argued in his own defense before being arrested. "I studied under Gamaliel and was thoroughly trained in the law of our ancestors. I was just as zealous for God as any of you are today" (Acts 22:3).

Furthermore, remember that when Paul spoke of Jewish dogs, he was not speaking of an entire race of people. He was speaking of a specific group of folks: his Israelite kinsmen who were distorting the gospel. In fact, he was speaking to his *fellow Judeans*. Paul was criticizing his own people, the people he grew up around, the people with whom he had the greatest social connection and influence. He did not share their religious perspectives, but he was an insider. He was, more accurately, an insider with an outsider perspective. That means at some level he was able to speak to Judeans in a way that no one else would have been able to speak to them. He knew the hot-button issues, the local values. This insider status gave Paul special opportunities, but it also made him the object of particular scorn. The Judeans, for their part, weren't thrilled about this rabble-rouser. These were the folks who opposed Paul, got him arrested and eventually got him killed. Although Paul can be accused of being very angry and even of name calling, he is not racist—neither by ancient nor modern standards.

Conclusion

Let us be very clear about one thing: this may be one of those times it is best not to imitate Paul. We would not suggest that anyone incorporate racially insensitive language into personal or public discourse in an effort to enhance discipleship. If Paul were in ministry in the United States in the twenty-first century, we believe he'd avoid hurtful racial stereotypes and opt instead for rhetorical strategies more suited to his audience. Likewise, although Paul preached on street corners in his day (as other philosopher-teachers did), we don't recommend street preaching today. Cultures have changed and Paul had a knack for adapting his strategies for the sake of the gospel (1 Cor 9:22-23). Nevertheless, whatever strategy he might employ today, we suspect he'd still make everyone uncomfortable.

In the final analysis, though, the charge of racism against Paul turns out to be *reductio ad Hitlerum*. Accusers of Paul connect him to Hitler in three moves (through Luther) and then hang the albatross of anti-Semitism around Paul's neck where it doesn't belong. Christians through the centuries have been guilty of heinous racism in general and anti-Semitism specifically, and unfortunately they have summoned the writings of Paul as supporting evidence. However, in recent years the racist charge against Paul has largely vanished and his writings have been used to show that Christians should be leading the charge against racism because of the gospel. Just look at Paul's cross-cultural ministry and you see at once the power of Christ to transcend the cultural boundaries of race and ethnicity.

The people of Israel, the descendants of Abraham, were God's chosen people and believed that unless a person became an Israelite, they could not participate in God's covenant. They considered Gentiles beyond the scope of God's salvation. In fact, the Jews (especially the Judeans) of Paul's day despised Gentiles. The feeling was often mutual. Despite the disapproval of his countrymen, Paul considered himself the "apostle to the Gentiles" and referred to himself that way often (Rom 1:5, 11:13; Gal 2:8). Paul consistently rejected the Jews' point of view in his letters. God did something new in Christ, Paul argued, and made it possible for Gentiles to enter God's covenant and experience his salvation by faith just as they are. "There is no difference between Jew and Gentile," Paul maintained, "for all have sinned and fall short of the glory of God, and all are justified freely by his grace through the redemption that came by Christ Jesus" (Rom 3:22-24). Again, we read the terms "Jew" and "Gentile" as racial indicators, but in Paul's day these terms were also religious and geographical terms. Paul is saying the place and religion into which one is born doesn't matter. All have sinned and all are saved by grace. Ethnicity/religion doesn't give Jews any more access to God's grace, nor does ethnicity/religion give Gentiles any less access to God's grace. "For we were all baptized by one Spirit so as to form one body—whether Jews or Gentiles, slave or free—and we were all given the one Spirit to drink" (1 Cor 12:13). Paul wanted to be sure Gentile believers never felt like second-class citizens in God's kingdom.

Paul wanted the Gentiles to be certain that God didn't view his church as two different congregations: a first-class Jewish one and a second-class Gentile one. And because God saw the two groups as one in Christ, Paul urged them to behave as if they were one. To the believers in Corinth, he said there should be no divisions. "One of you says, 'I follow Paul'; another, 'I follow Apollos'; another, 'I follow Cephas'; still another, 'I follow Christ'" (1 Cor 1:12). Paul was likely indicating the existence of house churches that are segregated ethnically.[10] The "Apollos" church was likely composed of Hellenized Jews for which Alexandria (Apollos's home) was well known. This group spoke Greek and interpreted Scripture in some interesting ways (largely allegorically). The "Cephas" church was likely composed of Palestinian Jews. We should note that they did not use the disciple's Greek name (*Petros*) but his Aramaic one (*Cephas*). Likely they spoke Aramaic in that congregation. The "Paul" church was likely where Gentiles felt most at home. Who knows what the "Christ" church was like. But it is easy to see how language differences would tend to sift folks. Paul was eager to remind his flock that their ultimate allegiance was to Christ, not to their ethnic group.

This was a more radical claim in Paul's day than it is in ours. This vision of a unified people made up of Jews and Gentiles was so radical, in fact, that Paul considered it his "special responsibility" to share it with the world (Eph 3:2 NLT). Remarkably, this insight was "not made known to people in other generations," but in Christ "it has now been revealed by the Spirit to God's holy apostles and prophets" (Eph 3:5). As far as Paul was concerned, the gospel of Christ made Jews and Gentiles equal—not the *same*—and brothers and sisters in Christ, children of God, heirs of the promise. And sometimes it's brothers and sisters, the ones who love you the most, who use the strongest language for your good.

four

PAUL SUPPORTED SLAVERY

In his autobiography of his life as a slave, Frederick Douglass tells a story about one of his masters who "experienced religion" at a Methodist camp meeting. Before he became a Christian, Captain Auld was cruel and cowardly, "destitute of every element of character commanding respect." Because Captain Auld started so low on the morality scale, Douglass "indulged a faint hope" that finding faith would make his master a better man. Maybe he would emancipate his slaves. If not, surely he would treat them more kindly.

Conversion worked a change in Captain Auld alright, but not the kind Douglass hoped for. Instead of making him a better man, becoming a Christian made him worse. "Prior to his conversion," Douglass writes, "[Auld] relied upon his own depravity to shield and sustain him in his savage barbarity; but after his conversion, he found religious sanction and support for his slaveholding cruelty." One vivid example illustrates Douglass's point:

> I have seen him tie up a lame young woman, and whip her with a heavy cowskin upon her naked shoulders, causing

> the warm red blood to drip; and in justification of the bloody deed, he would quote this passage of Scripture—"He that knoweth his master's will, and doeth it not, shall be beaten with many stripes."[1]

The first time I (Brandon) read this account, it made me sick to my stomach. As a human being, I'm horrified by the knowledge that another human being endured the agony and humiliation of such savage treatment. As a Christian, I'm doubly horrified to hear that someone could inflict such horror in the name of Jesus, with Scripture on his lips. The Jesus I know would never condone this behavior. Nor would the Peter or James or Paul I know.

And yet—and *yet*—Douglass's story is not so surprising to many modern Americans. Many today blame Christianity for strengthening the institution of slavery in the United States before the Civil War, and for good reason. There have been too many Captain Aulds among us, cruel men who have used Scripture as a crutch to support their cruelty. Worse, though, is that there have been many good, decent, godly men and women throughout history who were not *cruel* masters but who were masters nonetheless. These otherwise goodhearted, God-fearing men and women argued that the institution of slavery was established by God and that to oppose it, as the abolitionists did, was to strive against God himself. Even as popular opinion began to turn against chattel slavery in the nineteenth century, Christian ministers in the South insisted that God established the institution in the past and "he was not less wise and good then than now. The advancement of the world has not enlightened the mind, nor refined the sensibilities of deity."[2] According to many Christians in the Southern United States, no matter how the opinions of human beings may change, God stood and stands firmly behind the institution of slavery.

Reach back even further in history and you find Christians defending slavery almost from the very beginning. The Didache, a catechetical document that may have been written in the late first century, assumes slavery is a God-ordained institution. "Slaves, be subject to your masters," the document reads, "as to a type of God, in shame and fear" (4:11). None other than Augustine of Hippo claimed that slavery is always a result of sin, that being enslaved is God's means of humbling and disciplining the disobedient. It would be easy enough to distance ourselves from these historical figures—they aren't biblical authors. The problem is, time and again, at the heart of these arguments in defense of slavery are the writings of the apostle Paul.[3]

What Did Paul Really Say?

In fairness to Paul, we have to ask whether these later interpreters interpreted him correctly. Paul does indeed say a couple of things about slavery we can all take comfort in. For example, in 1 Timothy 1:10 Paul includes slave trading in a list of evils that are clearly "contrary to the sound doctrine." There is that remarkable statement in Ephesians in which Paul proclaims the radical unity of all human beings in Christ: "There is neither Jew nor Gentile, *neither slave nor free*, nor is there male and female, for you are all one in Christ Jesus" (Gal 3:28, emphasis added).

That pretty much sums up the good news. Unfortunately, Paul never *condemned* the institution of slavery. And that's what we wish he had done. We wish that somewhere he had said, "It is morally wrong to own a human being." But he never did. What's worse, Paul talked about slaves and slavery a lot, as if it was the most normal thing in the world. In fact, Paul refers to "slaves" and "slavery" more than thirty times in his letters. That's an average of more than twice per letter. Worse still, he bosses slaves around: "Slaves, obey your earthly masters with respect and fear" (Eph 6:5). And he clearly considered slaves to be second class: "My point is this: heirs, as long as they are minors, are *no better than slaves*" (Gal 4:1 NRSV, emphasis added). Paul paraphrases Genesis 21:10 to support his claim that children of slaves should not be given the same rights as children of free people: "But what does the scripture say? 'Drive out the slave and her child; for the child of the slave will not share the inheritance with the child of the free woman.' So then, friends, we are children, not of the slave but of the free woman" (Gal 4:30-31 NRSV). Paul even appears to encourage slaves to remain slaves and not to pursue freedom: "Let each of you remain in the condition in which you were called. Were you a slave when called? Do not be concerned about it" (1 Cor 7:20-21 NRSV). He seems to brush off the plight of slavery, telling the enslaved to be good slaves: "Let all who are under the yoke of slavery regard their masters as worthy of all honor, so that the name of God and the teaching may not be blasphemed" (1 Tim 6:1 NRSV). This wasn't just a stray comment. Paul tells another group of Christian slaves the same thing: "Slaves, obey your earthly masters in everything; and do it, not only when their eye is on you and to curry their favor, but with sincerity of heart and reverence for the Lord" (Col 3:22).

Greco-Roman Slavery and American Chattel Slavery

Some have tried to acquit Paul on grounds that Roman slavery in the first century was categorically different from American chattel slavery in the nineteenth century. When we balk at Paul's defense of slavery, some say, we are reading our context into his; we are reading our experience with American slavery (which was horrendous) into Paul's experience with Roman slavery (which, at the end of the day, was not so bad). Attending to cultural context is the right instinct, and it certainly sheds light on this conversation.

Ancients could not imagine a world without slaves. Who would do the work? The ancient workforce was not made up of employers and employees. It had masters and slaves, patrons and clients. According to some estimates, as many as 25 percent of the inhabitants of the Roman Empire were slaves.[4] The institution was a normal part of Roman life and it was generally accepted as morally appropriate. It is true Roman slavery differed in important ways from later American chattel slavery. For one, Roman slavery was not race based. "Latins, Greeks, dark-skinned Syrians, black Ethiopians, and blond, blue-eyed Germans could be slaves together under one owner."[5] People became slaves as captives of war. Others sold themselves (or were sold) for service to pay a debt they couldn't afford to repay. Jesus mentions this aspect of the system in a parable: "The master ordered that he and his wife and his children and all that he had be sold to repay the debt" (Mt 18:25).

Another way Roman slavery differed from American slavery is that Roman slaves were not automatically doomed to slavery for life. Debtors were freed when the debt was paid, as Jesus noted ("until he should pay back all he owed" [Mt 18:34]). Roman law provided for the emancipation of slaves at age thirty. And unlike slaves in the antebellum South, a slave in the first century could be permitted to take "a second job." He was allowed to keep his earnings and use them to buy his freedom.[6] At first blush, this seems to greatly reduce the plight of slaves. Many modern Westerners have barely entered their working years at age thirty. Paul's world, though, lacked modern nutrition and medicine, making it a harsh place to age. According to the best estimates,[7] of children who survived birth about half died by age ten. Military service killed a lot of men in their twenties and thirties, as did childbirth for women. If someone survived these perils, they commonly lived into their sixties, assuming they avoided the many epidemics that plagued the ancient world.[8] The reality was that many slaves didn't live long enough to be emancipated.

A third distinction between American and Roman slavery related to education. American slaveholders worked hard to ensure their slaves received no education. Ignorance, they realized, was key to keeping slaves submissive and productive. But this wasn't necessarily the case for slaves in first-century Rome. Publicly owned slaves held considerable status. They along with some privately owned slaves could be better skilled or more educated than their masters, and it wasn't unheard of for a slave to be literate while his master was illiterate. But common household slaves and farming slaves were not educated.

Lastly, under Greek law, a slave was permitted to own property and even to live in separate quarters from his owner.[9] Marriages between slaves and other slaves or freed slaves or even free persons were "very common."[10]

Roman slavery was not like American slavery. The two were not the same. However, simply pointing out the differences between Roman and American forms of slavery does not get Paul off the hook. The truth is, Roman slavery was as horrific as the American system. Seneca was a Roman philosopher and letter writer who lived in Rome at the same time as Paul. He describes slaves serving dinner to their master, "a household at his dinner with a mob of standing slaves":

> The master eats more than he can hold, and with monstrous greed loads his belly until it is stretched. . . . All this

> time the poor slaves may not move their lips, even to speak. The slightest murmur is repressed by the rod; even a chance sound,—a cough, a sneeze, or a hiccup,—is visited with the lash. There is a grievous penalty for the slightest breach of silence. All night long they must stand about, hungry and dumb.[11]

Yet the slave's life was worse than standing hungry while your master gorged himself. It was worse than suffering beatings for coughing and disturbing the master's meal. Some slave jobs, such as working in mines, were "a virtual death sentence."[12] Watching wives and children sold away to others amounted to emotional abuse. Perhaps worst of all, the slave and the spouse and even the children of slaves were often sexually exploited. Having sex with a slave was not even considered adultery in Roman culture. Seneca paints a distressing picture of another slave at dinner

> who serves the wine, [and] must dress like a woman and wrestle with his advancing years; he cannot get away from his boyhood; he is dragged back to it; and though he has already acquired a soldier's figure, he is kept beardless by having his hair smoothed away or plucked out by the roots, and he must remain awake throughout the night, dividing his time between his master's drunkenness and his lust; in the chamber he must be a man, at the feast a boy.[13]

Roman slavery was no picnic, and everyone knew it. Paul knew it. Paul was around slaves all the time. His churches had slaves as members. The term "household" that appears in expressions such as "some from Chloe's household" (1 Cor 1:11), "the household of Aristobulus" and "the household of Narcissus" (Rom 16:10-11) included slaves. He addressed slaves directly in his letters. Paul wasn't ignorant of the perils of slavery. From our perspective that is the real problem with him: he knew the horrors of slavery and still did not condemn it. Many modern critics pile guilt on Paul by noting that Seneca sounded far more gracious than Paul. Seneca argued slaves were also "people,"[14] reminding a slave owner: "Kindly remember that he whom you call your slave sprang from the same [divine] stock, is smiled upon by the same skies, and on equal terms with yourself breathes, lives, and dies. It is just as possible for you to see in him a free-born man as for him to see in you a slave."[15] How we might wish that Paul had said such noble things.

You're Gonna Have to Serve Somebody

Paul didn't have a blind spot when it came to slavery. It won't help us to argue that Paul was ignorant of the evils of slavery or that we have the benefit of clear hindsight and he did not. Plenty of people in Paul's generation recognized the horrors of slavery, so it's safe to assume Paul did too. And that fact brings us to the truly remarkable thing about Paul's teaching on slavery: he saw the situation clearly, yet his favorite self-identification as a minister of the gospel was "slave of Christ."

If we want to understand Paul correctly, we have to understand that Paul didn't have an official position on the institution of slavery as such. Instead, Paul had a profound point of view on the human condition, which informs his view of slavery and helps put it in perspective. While Paul certainly discusses the institution of slavery, he talks more often about slavery in a spiritual sense. In fact, most of the time when Paul uses the terminology of "slave" and "slavery" and "slaving," he isn't talking about humans serving other humans. Most of the time he's speaking of humans serving a spiritual master of some sort. Before being transformed by the grace of Christ, Paul claims, the Gentiles were enslaved to idols and false religion (Gal 4:8-9). Even God's children, the Israelites, were enslaved by the law, so that whether a person was part of God's chosen race or not, he or she was in bondage to something (Gal 4:1-8). Paul describes the general human condition before salvation in Jesus Christ as being "enslaved to sin" (Rom 6:6 NRSV). Sometimes he lists specific sins by which people may be mastered: they can be "slaves to drink" (Tit 2:3 NRSV) or "slaves to various passions and pleasures" (Tit 3:3 NRSV). And following the rules and regulations of human beings makes us "slaves of human beings" (1 Cor 7:23).

This slavery brings death to both body and spirit. Jesus died and was raised so that we "may have life, and have it to the full" (Jn 10:10). Paul understood this. That's why he wrote, "It is for freedom that Christ has set us free. Stand firm, then, and do not let yourselves be burdened again by a yoke of slavery" (Gal 5:1). So it makes sense that spiritual categories for Paul would be slavery (in sin) and emancipation (in Christ); bondage on the one hand and liberty on the other. Well, sort of. Actually, for Paul there seems to be only one category: bondage. The question is to whom or what are we in bondage? Paul isn't in uncharted territory here. Seneca used the same illustration: "Show me a man who is not a slave; one is a slave to lust, another to greed, another to ambition, and all men are slaves to fear."[17] But where Seneca bemoans this fact, Paul embraces it.

In the same passages where Paul calls all people either slaves to sin or slaves to manmade religious rules, he writes that we should instead be "slaves of God" (Rom 6:22) and "Christ's slave" (1 Cor 7:22). But Christian slavery involves submission to yet another master: others. Paul self-identified not only as a slave of Christ but also "as *your* slaves"—slaves to other Christians—"for

Jesus' sake" (2 Cor 4:5 NRSV, emphasis added). He claims that all Christians should be slaves to one another: "For you were called to freedom, brothers and sisters; only do not use your freedom as an opportunity for self-indulgence, but through love become slaves to one another" (Gal 5:13 NRSV).

"Slaves" or "Servants"?

We don't like to talk about slaves and slavery. It's distasteful. This pattern carries over into our modern English Bibles. The Greek word *doulos* means "slave." Modern English translations commonly translate *doulos* as "slave" when the context is about the institution of slavery ("slaves, obey your masters") and when it's talking about spiritual bondage in a negative sense ("slaves of sin"). But more often than not, when *doulos* is used as a self-identification by Paul or other New Testament writers ("*doulos* of Christ," etc.), modern English translations will use "servant." Greek has a word for a servant who is not a slave, *diakonos*. So, why do we translate James 1:1 as "James, a servant of Jesus Christ" instead of the more accurate, "James, a slave of Jesus Christ"? Is it not because calling James a slave seems harsh to our modern ears? We're squeamish about the topic of slavery. We're uncomfortable using the word positively even when the Scriptures do it. In the modern world, the word "slave" cannot have a positive meaning. Ancients actually felt the same way. Seneca never applied the word "slave" to himself. He even refused to call himself a slave to God.[16] The word rankled him and still rankles us. Nonetheless, New Testament writers used "slave" in a positive way. Should we hide that fact? Disguise it in our translations? What are we missing when we do?

Paul's slavery imagery reaches back to Israel's experience as described in the Old Testament. Israel understood as well as anyone what it meant to be slaves. For four hundred years they toiled under the yoke of Pharaoh. In Egypt they were the slaves of a terrible master who used force and violence in the form of forced labor and infanticide to suppress the people. God delivered Israel from that bondage. But he didn't take them out of Egyptian slavery in order to make them completely autonomous, free agents. He delivered them from slavery in Egypt to make them *his* slaves. God repeats in Exodus, "Let My people go, *that they may serve Me*" (Ex 7:16; 8:1, 20; 9:1, 13; 10:3 NASB, emphasis added). In other words, in Egypt they were the slaves of a terrible master, Pharaoh. In the wilderness and beyond, they were slaves of a wonderful Master, Yahweh. Those were the only options available to them. Being "free" in the sense that we think of it—total, individual autonomy—was not an option. (All of Israel's problems, both in the wilderness and the Promised Land, stemmed from the people's refusal to recognize and accept the fact that God was their Master and they were his slaves.) The New Testament extends the image. The church, like Israel, is God's slave. And they are slaves of the most benevolent master conceivable: Jesus Christ.

As far as Paul was concerned, to be a human is to be a slave. Our modern understanding of slavery makes us squirm at that statement. Perhaps our readers wish we would write "to be a human is be a *servant*." But we will stick with the biblical language. In the famous hymn about Jesus preserved in Philippians, Paul calls fellow believers to "have the same mindset as Christ Jesus" (Phil 2:5). He describes Jesus' obedient decision to leave the glory of heaven for the humility of earth in order to redeem his people. He "emptied himself," Paul writes, "taking the form of a slave, being born in human likeness" (Phil 2:7 NRSV). For Paul *slave* and *human* are parallel descriptors; to be born human is to take the form of a slave. The same point is a little clearer in 1 Corinthians 7. This is one of those problem passages where Paul says a couple of things we don't like, so it's worth quoting him at length.

> Were you a slave when you were called? Don't let it trouble you—although if you can gain your freedom, do so. For the one who was a slave when called to faith in the Lord is the Lord's freed person; similarly, the one who was free when called is Christ's slave. You were bought at a price; do not become slaves of human beings. Brothers and sisters, each person, as responsible to God, should remain in the situation they were in when God called them. (1 Cor 7:21-24)

Paul tells slaves not to fixate on freedom. "Don't let it trouble you," he says. He explains why in verse 22. If you are a slave

Slaves, Make Use of Your . . .

1 Corinthians 7:20-22 has a tricky part in verse 21. Paul says slaves are to make use of [something]. He doesn't state the object. Translations have to provide one. The option is either "slavery" or "freedom." The NRSV translators preferred "slavery," thus: "Even if you can gain your freedom, make use of *your present condition* [i.e., slavery] now more than ever." The NIV translators opted for "freedom," thus: "if you can gain your *freedom*, do so." The NIV is the better translation for several technical reasons.[18] Thus, Paul is telling slaves not to worry if they must remain slaves, but freedom is the preferred state.

(physically) when you become a Christian, you now belong—that's slave language—to the Lord. The same is true of masters. Even if they were free (physically) when they became Christians, they now belong to (are slaves of) Christ. Spiritually, then, both masters and slaves are equals, not because both are free but rather because they are both slaves of Christ. They were "bought with a price" (slave language again). That is, Paul doesn't argue that all humans are equal because we share an innate human dignity; he argues that all humans are equal because we are all slaves. We were not created to be free agents in the universe. The gospel of Jesus Christ offers us the most important freedom a human can have: the freedom to escape from slavery to sin into the service of Christ and to one another.

Paul didn't exactly hijack or redeem the imagery of slavery. Instead he embraced it because it was true. To be a human is to be a slave, but will you be enslaved to sin or enslaved to righteousness? Will you be enslaved to the power of darkness or to the Father of Light? Will you be enslaved to yourself, or willingly subject yourselves to others? Jesus taught the same lesson. You can't serve two masters—you can't serve [be a slave to] both God and money—but (we should not miss this point) you *will* serve someone or something. Paul couldn't imagine a world in which anyone was truly free. Even the rulers of the nations, arguably the freest men in the world, were ultimately God's servants (Rom 13:4). Paul would have agreed with Bob Dylan (on this point, at least), who sang, "It may be the devil or it may be the Lord, but you're gonna have to serve somebody."[19]

Perhaps this is one reason Paul doesn't argue clearly for the abolition of slavery. Paul is not nearly as concerned with social circumstances as he is with spiritual realities. Let's consider this odd paragraph from 1 Corinthians 7:

> Nevertheless, each person should live as a believer in whatever situation the Lord has assigned to them, just as God has called them. This is the rule I lay down in all the churches. Was a man already circumcised when he was called? He should not become uncircumcised. Was a man uncircumcised when he was called? He should not be circumcised. Circumcision is nothing and uncircumcision is nothing. Keeping God's commands is what counts. Each person should remain in the situation they were in when God called them.
>
> Were you a slave when you were called? Don't let it trouble you. . . . Brothers and sisters, each person, as responsible to God, should remain in the situation they were in when God called them. (1 Cor 7:17-21, 24)

Reading between the lines, the apostle seems to be saying that the gospel may not radically alter your social circumstances. In first-century Rome, one's status depended entirely on social circumstances. Masters were superior to slaves; men were superior to women; married people had more opportunities than singles. But becoming a Christian neither requires nor guarantees a change in social status. If you were single when you became a Christian, you don't *need* to be married, nor are you assured of a marriage proposal. If you were a slave, you don't *need* to be free, nor are you assured of freedom. Whether married, single, Gentile, Jew, male or female, the gospel does not necessarily radically alter our societal circumstances. But it *does* radically alter our relationships inside the church—all of them forever.

The Slave, He Is Our Brother

Nowhere is this truth illustrated more clearly than in Paul's letter to Philemon, a Christian in the church in Colossae. The backstory is this: Onesimus, a slave, ran away from his master. Philemon, the master, was a Christian and a disciple of Paul's. Onesimus was a Christian, too, and one quite dear to Paul. When Onesimus fled, he stayed with Paul, which meant Paul was housing a runaway slave. Runaway slaves were subject to extreme punishment. The way Paul handles the situation says more about his view of the institution of slavery and its implications than any other of his statements on the subject.

Under house arrest, living in an apartment in Rome, Paul had plenty of neighbors. In antiquity (like in a lot of the world today), everybody knew everybody else's business. His neighbors knew that a runaway slave had appealed to Paul to assist in his safe return to his owner. His neighbors would have expected Paul to do the "right thing": Paul should write a letter to Onesimus's owner, Philemon, telling him that his runaway slave had been found and that he should not execute the slave for running away but accept him back. That should be the extent of the letter. Yet Paul does more—a lot more—for Onesimus.

Paul makes the appeal personal from the beginning. He calls Philemon a "dear friend and fellow worker" (Philem 1). Likewise he calls Onesimus, the slave, "my son" and "my very heart" (Philem 10, 12). Paul instructs Philemon to accept Onesimus back without the expected beating. More than that, Philemon should accept Onesimus "no longer as a slave, but better than a slave, as a dear brother" (Philem 16). Although Paul has no legal rights over Onesimus or Philemon, Paul lays claims in the name of Christ and insists more. While we in the twenty-first century might critique Paul for not going far enough with Philemon, Paul's neighbors in the first century would insist that Paul had gone way too far.

Essentially Paul demanded that Philemon and the church at Colossae—and all Christians by extension—prioritize the new social rules of the church over the social rules of their society. Onesimus may retain the status of a slave in the broader Roman culture, but his social role within the Christian community was radically altered. In this way, Paul goes far beyond the teachers of his day. In his urging to Philemon, Paul is *subtle*. We may wish he was more direct, but the strategy is significant: If Paul was reinforcing the rules of society—keeping slaves in their place—why be subtle? Paul certainly had no trouble bluntly speaking his mind on other subjects. The reason Paul appeals to Philemon discreetly was *because* Paul was defying the norms of the institution of slavery. Tim Brookins argues Paul's term "no longer," in his command to welcome Onesimus "no longer as a slave, but better than a slave" (Philem 16), strongly indicates Paul was suggesting manumission.[20] Even if he wasn't, Paul challenged the Colossian church to recognize master and slave as spiritual equals.

A High-Stakes Gamble

Paul mentions Onesimus in a letter to the broader congregation in Colossae where Philemon, who was a wealthy benefactor, may have hosted the house church. More than that, Paul refers to Onesimus publicly as his "faithful and dear brother" (Col 4:9). All this puts Philemon and the church in an awkward position. If Philemon refuses to do what Paul asks, the church will be forced to decide which "father" to follow: their spiritual father Paul or their benefactor-father Philemon. In a very short letter, Paul has dramatically upped the stakes in the game.

Paul's comments to Philemon should influence the way we view other passages where Paul talks about slaves. Critics of Paul point out that Paul gave one verse of instructions to masters and four verses to slaves in his commands to the households in Ephesus and Colossae, suggesting Paul went easy on the slave owners. But addressing slaves at all was relatively radical: Greco-Roman household codes addressed only the masters, yet Paul includes slaves among those to whom he writes. Furthermore, most of the commands to masters were covered by the commands to them as husbands and fathers. Fathers are not to exasperate their children *or their slaves* (Eph 6:4, 9); they are to love their wives and treat them kindly, and they are to treat their slaves the same way. Furthermore, most of the comments to slaves would have been heard as warnings to the master. The slaves are reminded they are really "slaves of Christ" (Eph 6:6), a subtle caution about beating Christ's slaves, for it is the Lord who handles such matters (Eph 6:8). Furthermore, the command to the master is often missed in English translations: "And masters, treat your slaves in the same way." (Eph 6:9). In what way? The answer lies in the structure of Paul's command:

Slaves, . . . *serve* (v. 5) . . .
doing the will of God (v. 6)
serving the Lord and not men (v. 7)
knowing that each will receive back from the Lord (v. 8)
Masters, *do* the same things to them (v. 9)

Masters are to *serve* in the same way.[21] They are to submit to their slaves as an act of service to the Lord (Eph 5:21). This was an uncomfortable teaching—an all but unfathomable teaching—in Paul's day, too. While Seneca insisted that masters not be overly harsh with slaves, Paul exhorts masters to remember that ultimately both slave and master belong to Jesus, their mutual master in heaven (Eph 6:9; Col. 4:1).

Even Paul's seemingly harsh statement, "Slaves, obey . . ." (Eph 6:5), is conditioned. How are they to obey? Slaves are to obey their masters *as they obey the Lord*. This is not obedience from fear of a beating, but joyful service. Though being a slave is a horrific fate, that condition does not preclude the slave from Christian obedience. Remember that slaves who happen to be Christians have no choice about *whether* they serve. Yet they do have control over *how* they serve—grudgingly or joyfully. With their limited freedom, Paul exhorts them to serve joyfully and in this way testify to Christ. The master, who has greater freedom to alter the circumstances, is called to a more radical obedience: embrace the slave as your brother; love him as you love your wife; nurture him as you nurture your child.

Paul Behaving Badly?

This is all still rather abstract. Bear with us another moment as we compare Paul's perspective on slavery to that of others in his day. At first glance Seneca appeared to suggest equality between a slave and master. Writing to a slave owner, Seneca states, "It is just as possible to see in him [the slave] a free-born man."[22] Seneca wasn't saying what it sounds like he is saying. He wasn't arguing for equality between slaves and owners. He was suggesting that a rare slave could exhibit such nobility that the slave could elevate his soul to the level of the master. Seneca *never* argued for the abolition of slavery. In fact, when it was suggested his teaching could lean that way, Seneca sets the record straight. Slaves are to respect their masters. He writes, "I bid slaves respect their masters instead of fearing them. They say: 'This is what he plainly means: slaves are to pay respect as if they were clients or early-morning callers!' Anyone who holds this opinion forgets that what is enough for a god cannot be too little for a master."[23] Seneca was not overturning societal structures. Seneca, like Paul, could not envision a world without slavery.[24] But the two couldn't have disagreed more.

Seneca appealed to the Stoic understanding that all humans may be equal in their souls but some are suitable for freedom and others for slavery. Paul doesn't share the view that slavery is simply the way nature intended. Instead Paul radically reimagines the relationship between masters and slaves. Slaves and masters both share at the Lord's table. Recall Seneca's description of the slaves' role at their master's meal. Roman society dictated that slaves stand silently and watch as their masters ate. But the gospel of Christ dictated that masters and slaves share the meal together as equals. This simple truth has profound implications, especially in the ancient world that was quite particular about who ate with whom. Table fellowship was a consistent ethic for Paul. He demanded that Jews eat with Gentiles and that masters eat with slaves. This was a quiet sort of insurrection in the early church.

A shared table forces other changes. Paul was behaving badly (in ancient eyes) because he was arguing that in Christ, societal barriers should disappear. At the Lord's table, there are no lines separating Jews from Greeks, men from women, owners from slaves (1 Cor 12:13; Gal 3:28; Col 3:11). Paul argued it was better to serve than to be served. Paul was indeed behaving badly on this issue. Today we accuse him of bad behavior because he was not as radical as we wish, but Paul was behaving badly in *his* day because he wasn't as conservative as his church members wished.

So although we may critique Paul because he never explicitly calls for the abolition of slavery, he argues Christians are under a new world order (the shared table of the Lord). He also does more than other writers of his day, such as Seneca, who suggested that slavery was a matter of indifference to the enlightened soul; Paul notes freedom was preferable. When Paul advocates for the emancipation of Onesimus, he is not dismantling the entire institution. But it is clear that emancipation was on Paul's mind. Furthermore, Paul writes to two different churches that, in Christ and under the new dispensation of grace, "There is neither Jew nor Gentile, neither slave nor free, nor is there male and female, for you are all one in Christ Jesus" (Gal 3:28; Col 3:11). The hierarchies that apply in the world are null and void in Christ's church. While not unpacked fully, isn't this a tacit rejection of institutions like slavery, which presuppose the superiority of one class of people and the inferiority of another? Based on these passages, we might say that if Paul wasn't as clear as we would like for him to be, he was at least in the right boat and drifting toward the right shore.

Conclusion

In modern times, nearly the worst indictment critics can level at a position or movement is to say that it is on "the wrong side of history." Critics of Paul argue that because he never advocated for abolition or the civil rights of slaves, Paul and the Christian church he founded are on the wrong side of history. But this oversimplifies the facts.

To begin with, in Paul's generation the Christian church didn't have the social clout to end Roman slavery. There were no ballot amendments or midterm elections. Christians didn't have the authority to overthrow a corrupt system. What was within their power was to love one another within those social systems with such pure and godly love that it gutted those systems of their power to oppress. Some still object, asking why Paul didn't at least demand that all Christian masters emancipate their slaves. It's the natural question, but it amounts to asking why Paul didn't invent an entirely new economic system for the Roman Empire. In that era, there weren't employers and employees; there were masters and slaves. Emancipated slaves could not attend a vocational school to develop new marketable skills; many freed slaves ended up in bondage to a new master, working in prostitution, or chose to live the rest of their lives in the home of their master. Judging Paul for not advocating for emancipation is judging him for not having the imagination to think up a social system that was impossible at the time.

We have more options available to us today. While we tsk, tsk at Paul for not doing more to improve the plight of slaves with his limited options, we might ask if we ourselves have leveraged the greater resources at our disposal to advocate for the migrant worker, house the refugee or rescue the victims of human trafficking.

Additionally, this critique ignores the radical new relationships Paul called believers to forge within existing systems. For Paul, human servitude was a physical analogy of a spiritual reality. In the local church, Paul saw that both slaves and masters abused the institution as the more immediate problem with slavery. Paul commanded slaves to submit to their masters because, whether we like it or not, submission is an important spiritual discipline. The obedience required for being an obedient slave was the same obedience required for being a good Christian. In the same way, the benevolence of a good master is an image of the gracious care of our Master, Jesus Christ. For both masters and slaves, they were to serve each other and the Lord. We can criticize Paul for not unpacking the full impact of what these new rules would mean, but do we also fault Paul for not working through every implication of the gospel, especially when it was probably outside his wildest imagination? "Paul's theology was not a fixed body of thought, but a work in progress."[25] He laid the correct foundation: "There is . . . neither slave nor free . . . for you are all one in Christ Jesus" (Gal 3:28).

That brings us to the last point. Paul clearly planted seeds that flourished into abolition centuries after his death. If the church failed to water and cultivate these seeds, and it did, Paul is not to blame. Paul's language about slaves seems woefully behind the times. But that's easy for us to say on *this* side of history. To those of us who are further along in history, the people behind us will always appear "behind the times." This can be said of any pioneer, including scientists. We don't criticize Newton for having an insufficient understanding of physics. We say he knew more than anyone else at the time. But when the issue is moral, not scientific, we have different standards. We judge based on all we've learned. When you get to Z, it's easy to look back at Y and think that Y looks restrictive. But we have to look back historically and remember that Y is what got us from X to Z in the first place. We feel like Paul was behind the times because we have closed the discussion on slavery. That issue is an issue of the past, and Paul's arguments are a relic of the past.

For Christians, it is a mistake to relegate Paul's discussion on slavery to the past. To do so would imply that Paul's ethic carries no imperative for us today. We want to remove "slavery" from Paul's language when what we ought to be doing is inserting it into ours. As is so often the case, the world has things upside down. "But now that you have been set free from sin and have become slaves of God . . ." (Rom 6:22). Paul is saying, *Don't fool yourself—none of you is free, not the way you think of freedom.* The difference between Paul and Seneca is the same as the difference between Paul and the modern spirit. When Seneca spoke of equality between slaves and masters, he was arguing for lifting a (rare) slave to the level of a master. This is the direction we want to move: up. And we feel obliged to take people with us. Paul, in contrast, argues Christians should voluntarily lower themselves to the level of a servant (slave), following the example of Christ who lowered himself and took on the form of a servant (slave). Believers should do likewise.[26] While the world advocates for social ascension, the gospel calls us to follow Christ in downward mobility.

five

PAUL WAS A CHAUVINIST

The General Synod of the Church of England met in February 2014 to advance policies that would pave the way for ordaining women as bishops. In November of that year the church approved the necessary legislation and in January 2015, Libby Lane was ordained as the first-ever female bishop in the Church of England. But the whole affair started with a palpable irony when, in that February 2014 meeting, the proceedings began with the required lectionary readings for the day. The New Testament reading that opened the meeting to determine the future of female bishops was 1 Timothy 2:11-14: "A woman should learn in quietness and full submission. I do not permit a woman to teach or to assume authority over a man; she must be quiet. For Adam was formed first, then Eve. And Adam was not the one deceived; it was the woman who was deceived and became a sinner."

One observer summarized the lesson of the proceedings in this way:

> It is perhaps unsurprising, then, that so many people with modern liberal values are rejecting the church, unable to

> square their own sense of what's right and wrong on issues like gender and sexuality with teachings taken from a book written over a thousand years ago. The irony is that the church is increasingly being seen, no longer as a repository for ethical guidance, but as a force for immorality in society.[1]

Inside the church and outside of it, many modern readers are coming to a similar conclusion. Particularly when it comes to gender and sexuality, many view the church as repressive and oppressive. This view isn't new. Randy keeps a quotation from Sarah Grimké on his office door to prompt his male students to consider how they treat their female colleagues: "I ask no favors for my sex. I surrender not our claim to equality. All I ask of our brethren is, that they will take their feet from off our necks, and permit us to stand upright on that ground which God designed us to occupy."[2] These are sentiments from 1837 that resonate today. Ms. Grimké, a devoted Christian, believed the Scriptures offered equality to women but that Christian men ignored the Bible's teachings. A growing number today feel perhaps the Bible itself is the problem. There are statements in the writings of Paul that can be interpreted to mean that even at their most virtuous, women are still less virtuous than men. In other words, Paul seems to imply that women aren't just the weaker sex; they may be the *lesser* sex. Many attempt to quickly redeem these words of Paul's, suggesting that although Paul might believe that women are weaker in some categories, they ultimately have their own, complementary strengths. But when many read Paul, they argue that Paul believes that women are part and parcel *lesser*.

To be fair, those who suggest Paul was a chauvinist are not without argument. It is Paul himself who says outrageous things such as the man stands just one notch below Christ; the woman stands *two* notches below. Men are saved by Jesus. Women are saved by childbirth.

From our modern vantage point, it seems Paul has different expectations for men and women both in the church and at home. More to the point, when we consider Paul's writings at face value, it appears that Paul has *lower* expectations for what women are capable of. So what does Paul *really* think about women?

Are Women Lesser in Virtue?

Paul offers instructions for corporate worship in 1 Timothy 2, a discussion that begins with a brief theology of prayer. "Petitions, prayers, intercession and thanksgiving [should] be made for all people—for kings and all those in authority," Paul explains, because God "wants all people to be saved and to come to a knowledge of the truth" (1 Tim 2:1-4). In order for this to happen, Paul exhorts, "I want the men everywhere to pray, lifting up holy hands without anger or disputing" (1 Tim 2:8). What a beautiful testimony those prayers of godly men will be to the love of God for all mankind!

And that's where the conversation veers strangely in a new direction. "I also want the women to dress modestly," Paul continues, "with decency and propriety, adorning themselves, not with elaborate hairstyles or gold or pearls or expensive clothes, but with good deeds, appropriate for women who profess to worship God" (1 Tim 2:9-10). It's hard to understand how Paul's concern for the way women dress relates to his view of prayer and God's desire for people to be saved. If God wants all people to be saved, then the men must pray and the women must dress modestly? Really? This suggests Paul has a radically lower expectation for the women. The men are about the work of God. The women are about fashion (or lack thereof). The men have great capacity for prayer. The women have great capacity for vanity. Men should concentrate on prayer; women should concentrate on their wardrobe.

The impression that Paul views women poorly grows when you consider the way he talks about requirements for those who serve in ministry. First Timothy 3 contains one of Paul's longer treatments on the qualifications for overseers and deacons. A deacon is to be

> above reproach, faithful to his wife, temperate, self-controlled, respectable, hospitable, able to teach, not given to drunkenness, not violent but gentle, not quarrelsome, not a lover of money. He must manage his own family well. . . . He must not be a recent convert. . . . He must also have a good reputation with outsiders. (1 Tim 3:2-7)

Deacons receive a somewhat shorter treatment. But women receive the briefest. "In the same way," Paul writes, "the women are to be worthy of respect, not malicious talkers but temperate and trustworthy in everything" (1 Tim 3:11). Respectability, temperance and trustworthiness are familiar qualifications. Paul demands those from overseers and deacons too. But there's a new requirement here: women can't be "malicious talkers." The Voice translation calls them "backstabbing gossips." The NRSV uses "slanderers." Paul seems to single out women, not men, as having a hard time controlling their tongues. What a chauvinistic stereotype this seems to be. Women can serve if they can hold their tongues—*but I doubt they can.*

The apostle's estimation of women seems even lower when he writes to Titus, where he gives counsel about choosing church leaders. Paul instructs Titus to teach the other men to be "temperate, worthy of respect, self-controlled, and sound in faith, in love and in endurance" (Tit 2:2). Admirable qualities, all. The women, by contrast, are encouraged to "be reverent in the way they live, not to be slanderers or addicted to much wine, but to teach what is good." Their chief role is to teach "the younger women to love their husbands and children, to be self-controlled and pure, to be busy at home, to be kind, and to be subject to their husbands, so that no one will malign the word of God" (Tit 2:3-5). Men are expected to be examples of love and endurance, while the best we can hope for women is that they won't gossip and that they teach younger women how to keep their place in the home. In other words, men are expected to be "sound in faith," and women are expected to be sober. And "sober" isn't metaphorical—it means they shouldn't be alcoholics.

Taken together, these statements of Paul's give the impression that he views women as generally weak-willed. They are vain and conceited and show off with their clothes. They have a hard time controlling both their tongues and their alcohol consumption. Granted, loose tongues do tend to accompany booze, but that's as true for men as for women. In 1 Timothy 5 Paul implies women can't control their sexual passions, either. Paul tells Timothy not to bother supporting the younger widows in the church financially, because "when their sensual desires overcome their dedication to Christ, they want to marry" (1 Tim 5:11). All in all, this isn't a flattering portrait of women. The images that comes to mind are the Real Housewives from some reality TV show. They show up in their form-fitting skirts, drink too much, spout off, and before you know it somebody gets punched in the nose.

If Paul portrayed men and women alike this way, we might excuse him. We might chalk up the description as hyperbole. But he doesn't. He seems to suggest that women have a lower capacity than men for virtue. They are less likely to practice self-control, less likely to love their neighbor, less likely to be concerned about the things of God.

ARE WOMEN LESSER IN INTELLIGENCE?

In addition to being inferior to men in their capacity for virtue, Paul seems to suggest women are also inferior to men in their intelligence. Paul warns Timothy about false prophets and charlatans who will proliferate in the "last days," men who take advantage of others to improve their own situations. These foul people are "lovers of money, boastful, proud, abusive, disobedient to their parents, ungrateful, unholy," regular scumbags (2 Tim 3:2). But in his warning against these people, he inadvertently insults the women. These wicked men, Paul explains, "are the kind who worm their way into homes and gain control over gullible women." If that weren't enough, these "gullible women" are "loaded down with sins and are swayed by all kinds of evil desires" (2 Tim 3:6). We return, then, to the charge that Paul views women as less capable than men of exercising virtue. But maybe here we've discovered the reason. Women struggle with sin because their feeble minds are easily led into error.

In a couple of other places, Paul addresses the same issue a little more directly. Consider these instructions to the women of Corinth:

> Women should remain silent in the churches. They are not allowed to speak, but must be in submission, as the law says. If they want to inquire about something, they should ask their own husbands at home; for it is disgraceful for a woman to speak in the church. (1 Cor 14:34-35)

Paul silences women in another passage as well—"a woman should learn in quietness and full submission"—but adds a theological justification for the prohibition. The reason a woman must be quiet in church, Paul explains, goes all the way back to the Garden of Eden, to the creation of the first human beings. Women must be quiet because "Adam was formed first, then Eve." Moreover, "Adam was not the one deceived; it was the woman who was deceived and became a sinner" (1 Tim 2:13-14). In the first instance, it appears, women are not permitted to talk because the man has priority—he is first. The second instance appears to confirm what we've suspected in this section, that women are somehow flawed by virtue of being women. There it is: the problem with women is that Eve was deceived.

When Paul silences women in the church in Corinth, the context is an explanation of the proper order of worship. Paul explains, "Everything must be done so that the church may be built up" (1 Cor 14:26). Why would a woman's speaking in church not contribute to the building up of the church? Some scholars believe it's because women asked stupid, or at least elementary, questions that the men already knew the answers to. That's why Paul told the women to ask their husbands at home (1 Cor 14:35).

Are Women Lesser in General?

The good news is, "women will be saved through childbearing—if they continue in faith, love and holiness with propriety" (1 Tim 2:15). A man's hope is in the grace of Christ. A woman's hope is in having children and behaving herself. (That was sarcasm, in case you missed it.)

Yes, it is easy to paint Paul as arguing women are the lesser sex because they have a reduced capacity for virtue and intelligence. But the most damning charge with Paul's view of women is that, on the face of it, he appears to view women as the lesser sex because they are, quite simply, *lesser*.

Fairly consistently, Paul suggests that women are derivative of men. Man (as in male) comes from God and woman comes from man. "I want you realize that the head of every man is Christ," Paul writes, "and the head of the woman is man, and the head of Christ is God" (1 Cor 11:3). The blow is softened by the fact that Jesus, who in Paul's theology is all-in-all, the Alpha and Omega, also has a head: God himself. But does that really make it better for women? It still suggests that women are sort of thrice removed from God. God is the head of Christ. Christ is the head of man. Man is the head of woman. Where men have a divine authority over them, women have a human authority over them. And women, it seems, do not exercise authority over anyone else, except maybe their own children. They *are* the bottom rung on the leadership ladder. If this is true, it makes women categorically different, lesser, than men.

"The Head"

Paul uses the term *kephalē* ("head"), which is a challenging word. It usually means "head as in authority" but sometimes "head as in source." English tends to do the same thing. Brandon is the head of his school. The head of the Mississippi River is located in Itasca State Park. Some scholars suggest Paul meant "source" and is referring to Genesis. After all, Eve came from Adam. Before you breathe too heavy a sigh of relief, this creates its own problems: Did Christ come from God?

Just a few lines further down, in a conversation about whether women ought to cover their heads in worship, Paul goes on to say, "A man ought not to cover his head, since he is the image and glory of God." By contrast a woman "*is the glory of man.* For man did not come from woman, but woman from man; neither was man created for woman, but woman for man" (1 Cor 11:7-9, emphasis added). The logic feels strained. Men (as in males)—and only men—are made in the image of God and display his glory. Women, on the other hand, are made in the image of *men* and display *their* glory. Long before we resolve the question of how this applies to head coverings, it's clear Paul is describing some sort of spiritual hierarchy and that leaves women, once again, at the bottom.

Paul, Women and the Trajectory Hermeneutic

In the previous chapter on slavery, we argued that Paul planted a seed that grew into abolition, that even though he didn't end slavery he was moving in that direction. Those are two ways of saying the same thing: even though Paul did not articulate a complete or final statement on the issue at hand, his writings lay out a clear trajectory that makes it possible for us to decide how to apply his teachings faithfully in the present. This is called a *trajectory hermeneutic*. In order to decide whether that hermeneutic applies here, we need to describe the situation in the culture of Paul's day (X). Then we look at how Paul handles the situation (Y). Next we determine if there is movement, either in a more or a less restrictive direction. Lastly (and very importantly), does Paul provide a basis ("seed text") to suggest that the movement should continue in the same trajectory? If Paul's views of women are progressive for his times, does he offer texts that suggest we should offer women even more liberties than he explicitly mentions? If so, then this hermeneutical approach suggests that Christianity is expected to continue to move in that direction toward a Z that would represent our ideal stance (often represented in the seed texts). In other words, would Paul's handling of this issue look like this?

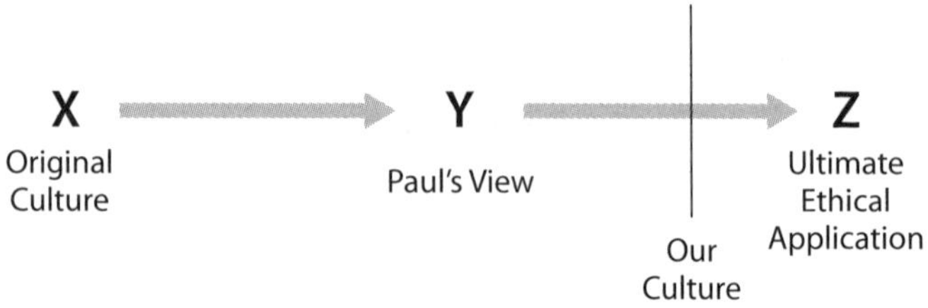

X → Y → Z

Original Culture | Paul's View | Our Culture | Ultimate Ethical Application

THE FIRST-CENTURY GENTILE VIEW OF WOMEN

Greeks and Jews rarely agreed but there was reasonable similarity in how they treated women. In an excellent study on women in the ancient world, Lynn Cohick discusses how women were viewed in Paul's day. Greco-Roman sources held up ideal virtues for the "wife." Her domain was the home, chastity was her virtue, and she was to be marked by modesty.[3] Poems, plays and stories served to reinforce the image of an industrious, dutiful, submissive wife. One particular story, oft-told but most famously by Livy, describes a dinner party attended only by men.[4] Once they were all drunk, the men began to brag about their wives' chastity. Before long they made wagers and then went home to prove their wives' virtue. To their disappointment, all but one wife was preparing to meet a lover when the husbands arrived home. The story illustrates both the *ideal* of the virtuous wife and the fear Roman men carried that, in fact, most wives were not virtuous. While we doubt this story represents the truth, it clearly demonstrates how Roman men viewed women: they were weak-willed and incapable of maintaining virtue without men to assist them. The charges overlap with some of the things Paul says about women in the New Testament, though we will notice important differences in a moment.

Change was in the wind in the first century. A small but influential group of women from the Empire's upper classes, sometimes called "Roman matrons," demanded and enjoyed a new measure of freedom. They received at least rudimentary education, free to be involved in social and even economic activity outside the home. They were in some ways the "liberated women" of the Roman world. Cohick demonstrates, for example, that women served in all levels of religious life in Roman culture, "from mere devotees, to simple ministers of cult sites, to high priestesses offering sacrifices on behalf of the empire."[5] The roles of women, while not clearly described, do indicate they held powerful positions and were often counterparts of male priests.

As you might imagine, not all Romans were thrilled about these changing social roles. "The wives of some of the Roman emperors during the period of the New Testament have been described as 'sensational.'"[6] But not in a good way. All this is to say that the place of women in Roman society was undergoing tumultuous change at the time Paul wrote. A few women were beginning to enjoy greater freedoms than Roman women had enjoyed before, though most retained their more traditional roles. What remained constant was the way Roman men viewed Roman women. Male writers generally disparaged the participation of women anywhere but in the home, describing them as "gullible, hysterical, and given to excesses in religious devotion."[7] Based on the detailed evidence Cohick amasses, there is little evidence to suggest this negative depiction of women was in any way true. But we can safely conclude that Roman men held Roman women in low regard.

The Jewish View

Josephus is often quoted as representative of the Jewish view of women in the Roman Empire.

> The woman, says the law, is in all things inferior to the man. Let her accordingly be submissive, not for her humiliation, but that she may be directed, for the authority has been given by God to the man.[8]

Josephus feels no need to justify his assertion. It merely represents the prevailing view of his time. Jewish literature contains numerous warnings against the lazy and wicked wife. As early as Proverbs we are told nagging wives are like a leaky roof (Prov 27:15) and that husbands are better off sleeping on the roof than to share a bed with quarrelsome wife (Prov 21:9; 25:24).

In Jewish writing from just before Paul's time, Ben Sira lists the sins of a wicked wife, exclaiming, "I would rather live with a lion and a dragon than live with an evil woman" (Sir 25:16). A woman's sins are simply worse than a man's. "Any iniquity is small compared to a woman's iniquity" (Sir 25:19). And a man's woes are a woman's fault:

> Dejected mind, gloomy face,
> and wounded heart come from an evil wife.
> Drooping hands and weak knees
> come from the wife who does not make her husband happy. (Sir 25:23)

She is noisy and disobedient instead of quiet and submissive (Sir 25:25-26). According to Ben Sira, we should not be surprised, for "from a woman sin had its beginning, and because of her we all die" (Sir 25:24). Grim. Craig Keener notes, "The rabbis clearly had it in for Eve."[9] In their thinking, women menstruated because Eve was responsible for Adam's blood. In funerals, women walked in front of the funeral bier because it was Eve who brought death into the world. In Jewish interpretations of Genesis written around the time of Paul, everyone in the story

(God, the serpent, Adam and even Eve) all recognize the fall of humanity was Eve's fault. It is fair to say that, like Roman men, Jewish men held women in low regard.

The question for us is whether Paul affirmed or challenged the cultural assumptions about women shared by men of all ethnic and religious backgrounds at the time. Was Paul the same or different? The passages of Paul that trouble us most can be boiled down to three general categories: the role women have in the church, their role in the family and the issue of spiritual hierarchy. Each of these subjects is complex—entire books have been written about each one[10]—and godly people who love both the Lord and Scripture strongly disagree on how to interpret Paul in each case. It might seem that we are oversimplifying this discussion, but our goal is not to offer the final word on Paul's teachings on women but rather to assess whether Paul is a chauvinist, either by ancient or modern standards.

A Woman's Role in the Church

As we have seen, three passages in Paul seem to restrict the roles of women in church: women must keep their heads covered when speaking (1 Cor 11:1-16), women should not interrupt church meetings with questions (1 Cor 14:34-35) and women should learn in silence (1 Tim 2:9-15). All three passages, taken at face value, limit the opportunity for women to speak in church.

Paul tells the women in Corinth they shouldn't speak in church, stating, "Women should remain silent in the churches. They are not allowed to speak, but must be in submission, as the law says" (1 Cor 14:34). That seems fairly straightforward. It reads as if Paul is telling *all* women and *only* women to be silent in church. Yet this passage isn't as clear as many like to paint it. In the *very same* letter Paul discusses the proper manner for women to speak and pray publicly in church (1 Cor 11:2-16). Obviously Paul expects and encourages women to speak *sometimes,* and this prohibition in 1 Corinthians 14 is not as broad as it at first appears.

Scholars are engaged in an important conversation about exactly how to translate some of the more confusing passages in 1 Corinthians. Sometimes it sounds like Paul is quoting his opponents' "slogans" and then responding to them. The challenge is that there are no quotation marks in Greek, so it is difficult to know where Paul's thoughts begin and his opponents' thoughts end. Modern translations take a stab at making the distinction by adding quotation marks and transition statements. For example, in the NIV 1 Cor 6:12 reads:

> "I have the right to do anything," you say—but not everything is beneficial.

Neither the quotation marks nor the phrase "you say" appear in the original Greek text. They are added to distinguish between a claim Paul is refuting and his own opinion on the subject. Returning to the matter of women speaking in church, some scholars suggest we need to insert quotation marks around 1 Corinthians 14:34-35. They argue that Paul does not prohibit women from speaking in church; his opponents do.

The problem is, the "clarifying" statement that follows the prohibition adds confusion. Paul says when they speak, women should have their heads covered; otherwise it dishonors the head. Instead of clearing things up, this statement introduces a whole host of exegetical difficulties. With what should they cover the head, with "long hair" or a marriage veil? Most women wore their hair long, and adult women (who were married) typically wore a veil in public. It may be that some women were treating the church service as a private home event (because the churches met in private homes, probably *their* home), and thus a situation where they were allowed to take off the marriage veil.

There was a law in Cyprus that a woman caught in adultery must have her hair cut off and must be a prostitute. Her shorn hair would publicly mark her,[11] the way the scarlet letter marked Hester Prynne in Nathaniel Hawthorne's novel. Some scholars suggest there was a "specific class" of rebellious women in the church who cut their hair as a sort of protest against laws like this.[12] Although it is possible that such a group existed and this is what Paul is addressing, it seems more likely Paul is talking about the marriage veil: "Paul equated not wearing a veil with the social stigma of a publicly exposed and punished adulteress reduced to the status of a prostitute."[13]

So was Paul fussing about hairstyles—Christian women were acting like those "shorn women"—or was Paul fussing because patronesses were treating church like their personal party? To add to the confusion, whose head is being dishonored? Paul only says "the head." If a woman prays with her head uncovered, does she dishonor her own head or her husband (who is "head" of the family) or Christ (who is "head" of the church)? We are confident the Corinthians understood what Paul meant, but we don't have enough details to be so confident ourselves. Before we get lost in the weeds, the key point to notice here is if Paul were forbidding all women to speak ever, then he wouldn't offer guidelines for the proper way for women to speak in worship. Clearly Paul was dealing with some specific situation in Corinth, whether shorn heads or unveiled women. The entire situation is awash in cultural customs that are largely lost to us.

Paul also argues women should learn in silence (1 Tim 2:11). In general neither Greeks nor Jews supported women learning.

Sotah 3 of the Jerusalem Talmud records a story of a woman asking a question about the Torah, which the rabbi refuses to answer on grounds that "a woman's wisdom is only in her spinning wheel." He goes on to say that he would rather "Let the words of the Torah be burnt and not given to women!"[15] When

Dressing Modestly

Cultural customs vary from age to age and place to place. Last Sunday, in hot South Florida, I (Randy) saw lots of godly women at church in sleeveless tops. My Indonesian Christian friends would have been aghast. They would argue, "Christian women must cover their shoulders!" For our part, we wouldn't approve of our Papuan Christian friends who don't trouble themselves with shirts at all. Even so, all three groups would appeal to Paul for support: "I also want the women to dress modestly" (1 Tim 2:9). As we have noted in another book, Paul was talking about *economic* modesty ("with gold, pearls or expensive clothes").[14] Paul was dealing with a specific situation—likely those troublesome, wealthy young widows. Paul's command certainly applies today. Women should dress modestly in church, not dressing in ways that say, "I have more money than you." Whatever the head-covering issue was about, it is likely Paul was addressing a socioeconomic problem and a propriety issue, not a gender problem.

we hang up on the detail that Paul wants women to learn in silence, we miss the broader and more radical point that Paul *wanted women to learn.* Paul advocated for the education of women in a culture that generally viewed education as the right of men only. Furthermore, Paul wanted women to learn in silence and in submission not because they were women but because that was the way *all* students were expected to learn in antiquity. The instructor's job was to speak. The student's job was to keep quiet and listen. Isocrates ordered Greek students to be silent.[16] Rabbi Akiba, a contemporary of Paul, likewise commended silence for learning. "The tradition is a fence around the Law; Tithes are a fence around riches; vows are a fence around abstinence; a fence around wisdom is silence."[17] Philo, a Jewish philosopher who lived in the early first century, describes sabbath synagogue proceedings in this way:

> [Moses] commanded them to assemble together in the same place, to sit with one another *with order and reverence* to listen to the laws, so that no one should be ignorant of anything in them; and, in fact, they do always assemble together and meet with each another [*sic*], *the majority mostly in silence*, except when it is appropriate to offer assent to what is being read.[18]

As this excerpt suggests, "silence" didn't mean utter and profound silence; it meant students should adopt a "quiet demeanor."[19]

While this might be outdated pedagogy, at least Paul didn't advocate beatings, which were also a common part of ancient education. Around the time of Paul, Quintilian noted, "I disapprove of flogging *although it is the regular custom*."[20] Quintilian was indeed the exception. When discussing Greek education, W. S. Davis noted, "When a boy has reached the age of seven, the time for feminine rule is over; henceforth his floggings, and they will be many, are to come from firm male hands."[21] Jewish education emphasized that sparing the rod would spoil the child (Prov 13:24; 22:15; 23:13; 29:15). Fortunately, we follow a different philosophy in our classrooms today. The point is, by ordering silence Paul wasn't treating women worse than male students; he was treating them *exactly like the male students*. This was true even of wealthy, elite patronesses who might have expected a higher measure of respect at church because the service was in her home. When it came to church, even the wealthy were expected to learn like any other student; there would be no preferential treatment just because they were meeting in her house and she might be paying the expenses. This practice might have earned Paul an accusation of not respecting the wealthy as they thought he should, but it would not have brought on the charge of chauvinism.

A Woman's Role in the Family

Paul instructs: "Wives, submit yourselves to your own husbands as you do to the Lord" (Eph 5:22). To be more accurate, Paul actually says, "Wives, to your husbands as to the Lord." There is no verb in the phrase because in Greek it is common to omit a verb if it is repeated from the previous sentence. The verb "submit" in our English translations comes from verse 21: "Submit to one another out of reverence for Christ." In verse 21, the verb is plural, so Paul is telling *all* Christians to submit to one another. Paul repeats the command for wives and then repeats the command for husbands: "Husbands, love your wives, just as Christ loved the church and gave himself up for her" (Eph 5:25). We misunderstand when we think Paul is giving a unique command to wives. Rather, for a reason likely clearer to the Ephesians than to us, Paul is emphasizing to Christian wives in Ephesus the importance of submitting. Bruce Winter argues that some of these women in Corinth may have been among those "new Roman women" who were casting off authority and moral restrictions.[22] It is possible that some women in Ephesus misunderstood Paul's law-free gospel and assumed he was advocating a similar movement. In response, Paul was stressing the essential Christian value of mutual submission under the lordship of Christ.

Hierarchy and Authority

The final category of Pauline passages about women has to do with how Paul ranks (for lack of a better term) men and women. There is no quibbling about what Paul *says* here: "For Adam was formed first, then Eve. And Adam was not the one deceived; it was the woman who was deceived and became a sinner" (1 Tim 2:13-14). Paul is arguing that Eve was weaker than Adam. Before all our female readers gather their pitchforks to come after us, allow us to explain what we mean. Paul argues that Satan tempted Eve rather than Adam because he considered Eve more easily tempted.

Eve may have been weaker than Adam, but this weakness didn't have anything to do with gender. Adam and Eve were different in two ways. First, Eve descended from a person—"man did not come from woman, but woman from man" (1 Cor 11:8); Adam was created directly by God, from the dust of the earth. Second, and perhaps more significant, Eve didn't receive God's revelation firsthand.[23] Adam received God's revelation directly from God, and he passed it on to Eve. God gives the command not to eat of the tree to Adam alone:

> And the Lord God commanded the man, "You are free to eat from any tree in the garden; but you must not eat from the tree of the knowledge of good and evil, for when you eat from it you will certainly die." (Gen 2:16-17)

After he gives Adam the command about the tree, God creates Eve: "Then the Lord God made a woman from the rib he had taken out of the man, and he brought her to the man" (Gen 2:22).

For Paul, it is significant that Eve was created *after* the initial revelation. Paul isn't concerned about gender. Rather, he's worried about *order*, sequence: "For Adam was formed *first*, then Eve" (1 Tim 2:13, emphasis added). This doesn't make *all* women second to *all* men. It only makes Eve second to Adam. After the Garden of Eden, all of us—male and female—stand with Eve. We were not created directly from dust. We did not hear God speak directly to us. Rather, like Eve, we come out of another human: our mothers (1 Cor 11:12). We hear of the command of God from another, including other people and even the Bible. We are all children of Eve. When Satan tempts Eve, *Did God really say . . . ?* (Gen 3:1), he is asking her to question both God and Adam. In the Genesis story, if Satan had asked Adam, *Did God really say . . . ?*, Adam would have answered, "He sure did. I heard him." Adam held a unique office. That's why Eve was weaker than Adam. But all of us since then, men and women alike, share Eve's weakness. How many of us hear the tempting whisper in our hearts, *Did God really say? Can you really trust the Bible?* Eve is second to Adam not in gender, but in sequence. You and I are also second to Adam.

This argument about the relationship between Adam and Eve and sequence may sound familiar. In his teaching about men and women in church, Paul essentially appeals to the logic the early church followed when they appealed to the authority of the apostles. The apostles were not ontologically better than other Christians. They weren't more spiritual because they were apostles and they weren't apostles because they were more spiritual. What set them apart was order, sequence. They were eyewitnesses to the story of Jesus. Everyone who believes the message of the gospel after them believes *because* of them—because they have preached it and passed it down to others who faithfully preach it themselves. We are not *lesser* than the apostles. But we do come *after* them. That is a critical distinction.

Evangelical Christians still strongly disagree about the role of women at home and at church. Typically the two camps arranged against each other are the egalitarians and the complementarians. Both views are held by wonderful Christian men *and women* who take Scripture very seriously. Their disagreements are usually over how particular texts should be interpreted. For example, when Paul forbids a woman to have authority over a man, egalitarians say he means "to exert authority" in the sense of "to domineer." Women should not be domineering. Complementarians, by contrast, insist the phrase means "to exercise authority" in the sense of a woman having spiritual authority over a man. That's why complementarians will insist women should not be pastors or, in some cases, teach men or older boys in any way. Reading the same material they draw different conclusions, but both hold the Scriptures and the truth of God in high esteem. "Exert" vs. "exercise" is a small but significant difference and these are important discussions that Christians should continue having, peacefully and respectfully. For the purposes of this chapter, it isn't necessary to choose a side on the specific discussion about women in ministry.[24] We are trying to honor the context in which Paul made his argument and the church positions that come most fiercely under debate did not exist in Paul's day in the same form as today. The significant point for the present discussion is that Paul's teachings about women were less restrictive than the contemporary teachings of both Jews and Greeks. Another way to say this is that whether Paul was an egalitarian or a complementarian, he was still more generous to women than just about anyone in his culture.

Saved Through Childbearing?

What are we to make of Paul's line about women being "saved through childbearing" (1 Tim 2:15)?[25] Since we are not sure if Paul is talking about all women everywhere or those pesky young (wealthy) widows in Ephesus, it is harder to figure out what this short, cryptic line means. If Paul was talking about the young widows wreaking havoc in Ephesus, sponsoring the false teachers and spending their days spreading trouble from house church to house church (1 Tim. 5:9-13), then likely Paul meant these women would be saved from the trouble they are in by getting themselves involved in more worthwhile activities—the same advice as the rest of the sentence (1 Tim 5:14-16). In this case, Paul isn't talking about "saved" in an eternal sense, but the more ordinary secular meaning of personal welfare. In fact, for a typical reader of Paul's day, "saved through childbearing" would refer to a safe delivery. Many, many ancient women died in childbirth. This does seem to be the more likely meaning, since Paul uses the future tense ("will be saved") and talks about love, holiness and modesty (a problem he noted repeatedly about these women).

Nonetheless, some suggest Paul is referring to all women because when Paul talks about "saved," he usually means eternal salvation not personal welfare. If Paul means women (as in all women everywhere) are saved through childbirth, then some scholars suggest Paul means "THE childbirth," referring to Jesus.[26] In other words, Paul is saying that although sin first entered the world through one woman's deed, salvation has come to the world through another woman's deed. One woman, Eve, helped get us in this trouble, but another woman, Mary, helped get us out. As we noted earlier, Eve is the prototype for all of us (males and females). She came from another human, as did we all (except Adam). She heard the revelation of God from another, as did we all (except Adam). Yet, Paul doesn't want condemnation to fall upon the female gender, for it was also a woman who brought our Savior into this world.

Seed Texts

If Paul is less restrictive than his culture in his teaching about women,[27] the question remains: Does Paul's position represent the endpoint of the trajectory? Has Paul outlined in his letters the extent of the liberties he believes women should enjoy? Or does he expect them to enjoy greater liberties in the future? Indeed Paul provides the "seed text" we need to answer that question. In Galatians 3:28, Paul writes, "There is neither Jew nor Gentile, neither slave nor free, nor is there male and female, for you are all one in Christ Jesus" (Gal 3:28). In previous chapters we have discussed the implications of this passage for race relations and the institution of slavery. We argued in both places that Paul was casting a vision of a radical new world order in which worldly distinctions that restricted access to God should be broken. Paul identifies the class difference between "male and female" with the class distinctions of "slave and free" and "Jew and Gentile." Paul argues there should be no ethnic inequalities in the kingdom of God. (Note: he doesn't argue there aren't ethnic differences.) While we have not yet achieved that goal, we at least see it as a goal to attain. Paul contends there should be no socioeconomic inequities in the kingdom of God, no slave or free, no wealthy or poor. We agree. Paul also says there should be no gender inequities in the kingdom of God. Most of us are not yet there. Nonetheless, this is the standard Paul calls us to.

In light of this, we would argue that Paul's view of women qualifies as a trajectory hermeneutic. Paul doesn't offer us the last word on the issue, but like his view on slavery, Paul has put us on a track toward a better ethic.[28]

WAS PAUL A CHAUVINIST?

We've done our best to defend Paul against the charge of chauvinism and we believe Paul should be acquitted. Nevertheless, some of the things he says certainly do sound chauvinistic, at least to twenty-first-century Western ears. If that's true for you, we suggest you keep a couple of things in mind when you read Paul.

First, remember that Paul's writings are "occasional writings." We have explained this before, but it bears repeating: all of Paul's writings are letters that were addressed to specific recipients to discuss a specific set of problems or questions. Some *occasion* prompted Paul to write each letter. Paul tells Timothy, "When you come, bring the cloak that I left with Carpus at Troas" (2 Tim 4:13). He also tells Philemon to prepare a guest room (Philem 22). These statements were directed at real, specific people in the past. When we read Paul's letters, we are reading someone else's mail. Because we only have half the story—Paul's response, but not the original question—we have to be very cautious jumping to conclusions. Paul points out to the Corinthians, who doubted the resurrection, "Now if there is no resurrection, what will those do who are baptized for the dead? If the dead are not raised at all, why are people baptized for them?" (1 Cor 15:29). We really don't know what Paul was talking about, but the Corinthians knew. We must practice a bit of humility when we pull statements from Paul and pronounce them as "Paul's view on women."

Second, because Paul's letter had original recipients (and we are not them), we have to be careful when we universalize Paul's statements that were intended as responses to specific situations. Paul saying that there were *some* gullible women in Ephesus is not the same thing as saying that all women in the world are gullible, or even that all the women in Ephesus were gullible. There were some gullible, weak-willed women in Ephesus sponsoring dinner parties for false teachers who were leading some church members astray. Paul steps in with a heavy hand because his church is in danger. But his response to specific women should not be extrapolated as his view of all women everywhere.

Finally, we have to be careful not to read the letters selectively and focus only on the statements that support or offend our sensibilities. It is indisputable that Paul had strong words for easily-deceived, weak-willed women who couldn't hold their tongues or their liquor. But focusing on these less-than-noble comments about some women can cause us to overlook that Paul praises and publicly acknowledges other women who served alongside him in ministry. In Paul's list of greetings at the end of Romans, he calls out Rufus's mom and Julia and Nereus's sister, who he calls "saints" (Rom 16:13, 15 NRSV). Paul identifies three female colleagues: Junia, who he calls "outstanding among the apostles" (Rom 16:7), Phoebe, a "deacon of the church in Cenchreae," and Priscilla who, along with her husband Aquila, Paul praises as his "coworkers in Christ Jesus" (Rom 16:1, 3). Indeed it is striking that everywhere Aquila is mentioned in the New Testament, his wife Priscilla is mentioned, as his coequal. Paul goes on to single out extraordinary women in the church of Rome: he refers to Tryphena, Tryphosa and Persis as women who have worked "hard in the Lord" (Rom 16:12). Some will argue that these women must have cooked and cleaned for him. We doubt it. Consider Paul's longer commendation of Euodia and Syntyche:

> I ask you, my true companion, help these women since they have contended at my side in the cause of the gospel, along with Clement and the rest of my co-workers, whose names are in the book of life. (Phil 4:3)

We should probably point out that these two women weren't getting along as well as Paul wanted (Phil 4:2), but that is true of plenty of men in Paul's letters. In fact, male workers in general get harsher rebukes from Paul. Nevertheless, we don't know exactly how Euodia and Syntyche contended at Paul's side, but they were active in "the cause of the gospel" and they are included in the company of "Clement and the rest of my co-workers."[29] At the end of 2 Timothy 4, several men are singled out for rebuke, but both men and women are included in the list of those Paul praises, leading us to understand his praises and rebukes as based simply on the deeds of each person.

Conclusion

Paul does indeed behave badly when it comes to women. His Jewish culture would not have been pleased with all the freedom and responsibility he suggested women had in Christ. Traditional Roman culture would have been equally displeased for the same reasons, and the modern "liberated" women of the day would have felt restricted by Paul's teachings.[30] Here at the end of this discussion, we find ourselves threading the same needle Paul threaded, urging an ethic uncomfortable to all parties involved for a variety of reasons. It is easy for us today to critique Paul for not going as far as we want—even though Paul is probably a key player in where we are so far. A glance at many contemporary non-Christian cultures, such as some Middle Eastern and South Asian cultures, offers plenty of examples to suggest that it isn't a

Christian background that is holding women back. After all, Western Christians don't debate whether or not it is appropriate to educate women. We take it for granted that it is. Western Christians don't debate whether women equal men in virtue or intelligence. Because of Paul's teaching on the inherent equality of men and women in Christ, we do not entertain serious debate about whether or not women are intrinsically *lesser* than men. Instead, we argue about which roles are appropriate for men and women, and many of those roles simply did not exist when Paul was writing. We find ourselves in agreement with Sarah Grimké again, though we might qualify the statement slightly: "Intellect is not sexed; . . . strength of mind is not sexed; and . . . our views about the duties of men and the duties of women, the sphere of man and the sphere of woman, are mere arbitrary opinions, differing in different ages and countries, and dependent solely on the will and judgment of erring mortals."[31]

One of the reasons we're talking about roles is because Westerners have restricted gender roles, far beyond what Paul ordained. Nonetheless, we are not where we want to be on women's rights. But is it fair to critique Paul, who lived two *thousand* years ago, for not being up to twenty-first-century standards?

Let us conclude by suggesting that we offer Paul the same grace we are hoping the next generation will offer us. While we feel like Paul didn't go far enough because we're still somewhere between Y and Z, our Christian sisters a hundred years from now will have plenty to critique *us* about. There is still a lot of room for improvement in how the church as well as our culture treats women. The question before us is how we will faithfully continue Paul's trajectory toward greater equality.

six

PAUL WAS HOMOPHOBIC

In 2015, the Supreme Court of the United States decided that the US Constitution gives same-sex couples the right to legal marriage, with all its benefits. Proponents of the legislation label it "marriage equality," calling it a landmark and long-overdue extension of basic civil rights. Its critics call it the beginning of the end of Western civilization as we know it.

The decision didn't polarize the nation; the nation was polarized on this subject long before. It did, however, force Americans to think in difficult binary terms. The decision was heralded by many as a victory for *civil* liberties and by others as a defeat for *religious* liberties. Culture and Christianity were set against one another in ways that are difficult to reconcile.

In such a climate, Christians want to be certain their position (whatever it may be) enjoys the support of Scripture. Given the certainty in many voices these days, it is somewhat surprising to discover that there are actually very few passages in the New Testament that address the subject of homosexuality directly. Jesus never mentions it. Some interpret his silence on the subject as implicit approval. Jesus denounced plenty of other sexual sins (e.g., adultery) but he never denounced homosexuality. Others interpret his silence as disapproval. The Old Testament law forbade homosexuality, and Jesus came not "to abolish the Law or the Prophets . . . but to fulfill them" (Mt 5:17). But arguments from silence are rarely conclusive. So if we want explicit New Testament teaching on homosexuality, we have to turn to Paul's epistles where even there we find very little. Paul broaches the subject only three times, in Romans, 1 Corinthians and 1 Timothy, and there he mentions homosexual behavior in the context of other sins as varied as drunkenness, stealing and talking back to your parents.

One commentator has argued that even though Paul includes homosexuality as one among other misbehaviors, homosexuality is nevertheless different from the rest. It is not like other sins, he writes, because, "At this moment in history, contrary to the other sins listed here, homosexuality is celebrated by our larger society with pioneering excitement. It's seen as a good thing, as the new hallmark of progress."[1] There again the conversation is framed as Christian conviction arranged against contemporary culture.

A number of Christians find it difficult to live with these options. *TIME* magazine reported in early 2015, "Support for gay marriage across all age groups of white evangelicals has increased by double digits, according to the Public Religious Research Institute, and the fastest change can be found among younger evangelicals—their support jumped from 20 percent in 2003 to 42 percent in 2014."[2] Many Christians today feel that surely we can reconcile our sincere Christian faith with a welcoming and accepting embrace of our gay and lesbian friends and family, especially those who profess Christian faith themselves. We understand. We have these conversations with questioning students and sincere seekers at the kitchen table, with neighbors and loved ones gay and straight. We suspect, for this reason, that readers are hoping for a clear and definitive statement from Paul that aligns with one pole or the other. (We suspect many readers turned to this chapter first, but we wish you'd go back to the beginning!) It turns out Paul's position falls in a middle ground that's sure to make all of us uncomfortable—or indignant—for different reasons.

Sexuality in First-Century Rome

Roman behavior was dictated by sexual mores that differed significantly from our own. On the one hand, first-century Roman ethics were much more permissive than just about anywhere in the twenty-first-century West. In Paul's world, Gentile men were expected to find both women and young men sexually attractive. The Roman poet and philosopher Lucretius (99–55 BC) wrote about the causes of sexual desire, being struck by the shafts of Venus's arrows "whether it be a boy with girlish limbs who launches the shaft at him, or a woman radiating love from her whole body."[3] Roman culture obsessed about "virility" (from the Latin word *vir*, meaning "a man"), and Roman men were considered "manly" whether they had sex with males, females or even children. Pederasty (literally "love of boys") had no immoral overtones in Roman culture, as long as the child was not freeborn. It was widely assumed, in fact, that one purpose of slave boys was to satisfy the lust of their owner. The Romans had favored terms for these boy slaves. A *puer delicates* ("boy toy") was a child-slave that a master used sexually, often calling him his *deliciae*, "sweets." This young boy, *delicatus* ("delicacy"), with his long hair and prepubescent features, was vulnerable and easily exploited.[4] The term *pusio* ("lad") was often used with sexual connotations. So pervasive was the appeal of young boys that Juvenal, in his *Satire* on marriage, suggested that killing oneself or getting a lad for a bed partner was preferable to marriage:

> Have you perhaps already given her finger your pledge? Well, you used to be sane, all right. Postumus, are you really getting married? . . . Can you put up with any woman as your boss with so many ropes available, when those dizzily high windows are wide open, when the Aemilian bridge offers itself to you so conveniently? Alternatively, if you don't like any of these many ways out, don't you think it would be better to have a boyfriend [*pusio,* lad] sleep with you? A boyfriend won't enter into nocturnal disputes, won't demand little presents from you as he lies there, and won't complain that you're not exerting yourself or that you're not panting as much as you're told to.[5]

Juvenal is of course satirizing marriage by suggesting it is better to jump from a bridge than to tie the knot. Even so, his suggestion to sleep with a lad was considered a quite acceptable alternative to heterosexual marriage.

Not only was a homosexual relationship considered entirely appropriate, it also was *not* considered adultery in Roman culture.[6] Amy Richlin relates the trial of a Roman man accused of adultery, which was considered immoral. The man's alibi was that he couldn't possibly be guilty of adultery, because he was having sex with a slave boy.[7]

Same-sex attraction was considered normal and healthy not only for Roman men but also for Roman gods. Charles Rowan Beye, a translator and scholar of ancient Greek literature, describes the Roman god Zeus in these terms: "Zeus is a male as well as a god. As a male, he is subject to the same needs that move humans. . . . So, Zeus *as a normal male* would have a strong erotic interest in good-looking teenage boys."[8]

There is even evidence of same-sex marriage in the first century. The Roman historian Tacitus relates the story of a very public imperial wedding ceremony in which Nero married his former slave Pythagoras. It is worth noting that this wasn't Nero's only same-sex marriage. He married another man on another occasion. But Tacitus shares this tale to shame Nero because, in this particular wedding, Nero was the bride:

> Nero himself . . . became, with the full rites of legitimate marriage, the wife of . . . Pythagoras. The veil was drawn over the imperial head, witnesses were dispatched to the scene; the dowry, the couch of wedded love, the nuptial torches, were there: everything, in fine, which night enshrouds even if a woman is the bride, was left open to the view.[9]

The description of sexual ethics in the first century so far paints a scene of absolute libertinism. This vignette from the life of Nero introduces some important exceptions. It would be inaccurate to say of sex in Rome that "anything goes." Although Roman culture was very accepting of homosexual behavior, it framed the entire matter differently than we do. While sexual urges of all kinds were considered entirely acceptable, certain sexual relationships were considered socially unacceptable. The Greco-Roman world didn't discuss sexuality in terms of "identity" or "orientation." It didn't use terms exactly equivalent to our "gay" (homosexual) and "straight" (heterosexual).[10] The Greco-Roman world differentiated not between gay and straight but between penetrator and penetrated.

Please excuse us for being indelicate, but in a discussion like this it is necessary for us to be very clear since euphemisms can lead to misunderstandings. A Roman man was expected to desire sex with both males and females as long as he took the dominant role. For Romans, this meant the role of penetrating rather than being penetrated.[11] Slaves or prostitutes (who were usually slaves) were acceptable partners for a Roman man *as long as* he took the dominant role.[12] Additionally, it was immoral (in Roman eyes) to have sex with a freeborn man's wife or an underage (thus unmarried) freeborn girl or boy. "Sexual intercourse with young slave boys is not only acceptable but normal; sexual intercourse with freeborn boys is deplorable and illegal, apparently for the benefit of the boy's pride and future reputation."[13] Freeborn boys were to be protected, not from homosexual activity per se but from being encouraged to take the role Romans considered "feminine" (that of being penetrated). Thus the story Tacitus told of Nero's wedding shamed Nero, *not* because it was a same-sex marriage, but because the Emperor was taking the submissive role.

To summarize, Roman culture was far more permissive than modern Western culture on issues of sexual morality. The Romans had scruples, of course, but they were very different scruples from ours. As they pertained to homosexual behavior in particular, Roman mores dealt in profound double standards. There are at least two important points to emphasize in this discussion, and both have implications for understanding Paul's position on homosexuality. The first point is that we are quite wrong to assert that homosexual behavior is either more tolerated or more celebrated today than it has ever been in the past. American culture's acceptance of homosexuality does not pose an unprecedented challenge for Christianity, as some have suggested in recent years. The second point is that it was precisely these Roman men, both freeborn and slave, both "active" and "passive" homosexual partners, whom Paul was winning to faith with the gospel of Jesus Christ. From a pastoral perspective, it is crucial to remember, as Paul did, that a convert's views on sexuality don't change overnight. Conversion doesn't instantaneously reorient all our opinions. That means Paul had church members who had engaged in all the behaviors described above. Perhaps some of them still did.

"Dishonorable" Sexual Activity in Rome

Actors and other entertainers were known as *infames* ("without honor"), partly due to their reputation for providing sexual favors to their patrons (by taking the submissive role). While there was no negative stigma at all for the *active* partner in homosexual relationships, Roman society humiliated the *passive* partner, often calling him *cinaedus,* a derogatory term difficult even to translate. We can see the humiliation in other terms:

> Here are some of the other names by which Romans called a sexually penetrated male: *pathicus, exoletus, concubinus* ("male concubine"), *sprintria* ("analist"), *puer* ("boy"), *pullus* ("chick" [an affectionate term for a small animal]), *pusio* ("lad"), *delicatus* ("exquisite"), *mollis* ("soft"), *tener* ("dainty"), *debilis* ("weak"), *effeminatus* ("effeminate"), *discinctus* ("loose-belted"), *morbosus* ("sick").[14]

A Roman man who desired to be penetrated was thought to have a "disease" (*morbus*), even though it was thought quite normal for a man to desire to penetrate another man or even a young boy.[15]

What Did Paul Say About Homosexual Behavior?

Paul mentions homosexuality only twice in passing and discusses it at length only once. In 1 Timothy 1:8-11, Paul includes homosexual behavior in a list of other behaviors he considers self-evidently "contrary to sound doctrine":

> We know that the law is good if one uses it properly. We also know that the law is made not for the righteous but for lawbreakers and rebels, the ungodly and sinful, the unholy and irreligious, for those who kill their fathers or mothers, for murderers, for the sexually immoral, for *those practicing homosexuality*, for slave traders and liars and perjurers—and for whatever else is contrary to the sound doctrine that conforms to the gospel concerning the glory of the blessed God, which he entrusted to me. (Emphasis added)

Similarly, in 1 Corinthians 6:9-10, Paul includes gay men in a list of those who will not inherit the kingdom of heaven:

> Or do you not know that wrongdoers will not inherit the kingdom of God? Do not be deceived: Neither the sexually immoral nor idolaters nor adulterers nor men who have sex with men nor thieves nor the greedy nor drunkards nor slanderers nor swindlers will inherit the kingdom of God.

Romans 1 is the epicenter for Paul's view on homosexuality. Paul argues that "God's invisible qualities—his eternal power and divine nature" are so evident in creation that everyone, even people who have never read the law of Moses or heard the gospel of Christ, stand without excuse for their ignorance (Rom 1:20). The Gentiles have ignored this revelation of God in nature and traded in the glory of God, the Creator, to worship created things instead. As a consequence of this rebellion,

> God gave them over to shameful lusts. Even their women exchanged natural sexual relations for unnatural ones. In the same way the men also abandoned natural relations with women and were inflamed with lust for one another. Men committed shameful acts with other men, and received in themselves the due penalty for their error. (Rom 1:26-27)

Essentially, Paul argues that the characteristic sin of the Gentiles is that idolatry has trumped love of God. Nowhere is this more evident than in human sexual appetite. In other words, homosexual behavior is a disorientation of a natural appetite. In Romans 1 it is presented as a visible manifestation of humanity's generally misplaced passions.

But it is not the *only* manifestation of misplaced passions. Paul continues in Romans 1 to say that these same people, the Gentiles, whose appetites are disoriented, are also "full of envy, murder, strife, deceit and malice. They are gossips, slanderers, God-haters, insolent, arrogant and boastful; they invent ways of doing evil; they disobey their parents; they have no understanding, no fidelity, no love, no mercy" (Rom 1:29-31). Even in Romans, where Paul gives the most attention to homosexuality, he includes it in a list of other behaviors that illustrate humanity's inclination to deviate from God's will.

The short and long of it is that Paul shared the Old Testament view of homosexuality—that it is sinful because it violates the law of God. Nowhere does Paul give the impression that the Old Testament's teaching on the subject is somehow out of date in light of the gospel. Paul was quite willing to abandon Old Testament prescriptions if he believed the new covenant superseded them. For example, Paul abandoned circumcision, a rite that was the central identifying marker of religious devotion in his Jewish heritage, because he considered it insignificant in light of the resurrection. "For in Christ Jesus neither circumcision nor uncircumcision has any value. The only thing that counts is faith expressing itself through love" (Gal 5:6). Paul lived in a culture that ate meat the Old Testament considered unclean and he told the Colossians not to let anyone condemn them for eating that meat (Col 2:16-22). If Paul had believed that homosexuality should be permitted under the new dispensation inaugurated by Christ, it seems that he would have said so. He had plenty of opportunity to say so. He lived in a culture that encouraged it and converted men who regularly practiced it.

Now while Paul endorsed the Old Testament's prohibition on homosexual behavior, it is equally true and equally significant that nowhere does Paul endorse the Old Testament *penalty* for homosexuality. Leviticus 18 calls homosexuality "detestable" and prescribes that anyone who practices it "must be cut off from their people" (Lev 18:29). Leviticus 20:13 says they should be put to death. Paul never suggests that churches round up all the gays and stone them to death. He never singles out homosexuals for church discipline by ostracism. He never questions the sincerity of the faith of church members who had in the past, or even still, kept gay lovers. He had plenty of opportunity to counsel all those things. It is almost certain that many of the earliest Gentile Christians had homosexual experience. Many if not most of the Christian men who were slaves were probably exploited as young boys. Slave owners routinely exploited their female and male slaves. They were a part of the Roman world and homosexuality was a normal part of that world.

PAUL BEHAVING BADLY

Although Paul never singles out homosexuality as a sin deserving of especially harsh judgment, neither does he affirm the behavior. For this reason, Paul likely offended everyone in his congregations for different reasons. By denouncing homosexual behavior, which was a perfectly acceptable part of Roman society, he behaved badly in the eyes of his Roman converts. Take another look at 1 Corinthians 6:9-10, where Paul includes "men who have sex with men" in a list of those who will not inherit the kingdom of heaven. If Paul had used the word for passive male partners in this verse, the Romans in the room would have agreed with him (and the Jews in the room would have cringed through the entire conversation). Of course, *those* men are detestable, the Romans would say. But Paul leaves no room for misinterpretation. In the Greek, Paul lists two Greek words: *malakoi* and *arsenokoitēs*. The first word literally means "soft" and referred to the man who took the passive role. The other word referred to the man who took the active role—the role the Romans admired. Paul considers both partners to be involved in shameful behavior. His goal was not to further shame the passive partner, who may have had no choice in the matter. His purpose was to challenge the Roman perception of morality. The virile Roman man who became a Christian was no longer free to express his sexual desires however he pleased. Paul was setting a more restrictive sexual ethic than his Roman converts would have imagined possible.

At the same time that Paul was setting a more restrictive sexual ethic than Roman converts found comfortable (or fair), he also extended grace to people the Jewish converts were uncomfortable embracing in Christian fellowship. Jewish converts in the churches would have been familiar with both the Levitical prohibitions against homosexual behavior *and* the Levitical punishment for that behavior. Their religious upbringing in Torah would have made it very difficult for them to believe that God could declare righteous anyone who currently or *had ever* committed acts their Scriptures clearly labeled egregious sins. When the letters we now call Romans, 1 Corinthians and 1 Timothy were originally read in the churches, the Roman Christians were likely embarrassed by Paul's prudishness about sexuality, but the Jewish Christians were likely scandalized by Paul's willingness to extend forgiveness and fellowship to sinners.

Sex with Your Spouse (Only)

Consider other of Paul's teachings on sexual immorality in light of this discussion. Many are familiar with Paul's encouragement, "But since sexual immorality is occurring, each man should have sexual relations with his own wife, and each woman with her own husband" (1 Cor 7:2). We would be right to assume Paul directed this command to an apparently promiscuous group. But we would be wrong to think Paul was only discussing adultery. American Christians would likely never dream Paul was telling husbands *in church* not to sleep with other men, young boys or slave girls. Or that Paul was commanding wives to limit themselves in the same way. Those kinds of behaviors were routine among Gentiles.

Unlike his Roman converts, Paul did not consider homosexual behavior any *better* than other forms of sexual misconduct; it was not an alibi for adultery. Unlike his Jewish converts (and many contemporary Christians), Paul didn't view homosexual behavior as any *worse* than other forms of sexual misconduct. Indeed, the other behaviors Paul lists when he mentions homosexuality—

arrogance, slander, gossip—are all equally damaging to the Christian community, and none of them are sexual. Our gay friends resent being lumped in with murderers and slave traders, as they are in 1 Timothy 1:8-11. We don't blame them. But notice that Paul also lumps gossips in with murderers. The point is Paul sees no hierarchy of sin. All sin is evidence of misplaced desire. We are made for loving companionship, and yet (in our sin) we undermine those relationships with power plays and backbiting. The family is made to represent Christ's love for the church, and yet (in our sin) parents exasperate children and children rebel. Paul's pastoral counsel for gay Christians would no doubt have been the same as for slanderers, thieves, adulterers and other Christians struggling to walk in the way of Jesus: "Do not conform to the pattern of this world, but be transformed by the renewing of your mind. Then you will be able to test and approve what God's will is—his good, pleasing and perfect will" (Rom 12:2). It likely doesn't occur to most modern readers that Paul is including homosexuality as behavior for committed Christians to "put off" (Eph 4:22).

And so we find Paul where we often find him: navigating the perilous terrain that runs between new pagan converts on the one hand and established, faithful religious folks on the other; navigating between a society's perception of justice and fairness on the one hand and a new world order that challenges the old system of righteousness by works. This gospel of Paul's was foolishness to the Gentiles because it was countercultural and counterintuitive. This same gospel was a stumbling block for the Jews because it threw open the gates of access to the throne of grace. Of course between these two poles we've just described, between libertinism and legalism, there lives a whole host of sincere believers trying to navigate this terrain with much less confidence than Paul possessed.

Is Homosexuality the New Civil Rights?

In our culture, it has been artfully and skillfully argued that when it comes to the issue of homosexuality, Paul is once again on the wrong side of history. This is a charge that merits a thoughtful response. We have already shown that we don't think Paul was wrong about women or slaves. While he doesn't campaign for emancipation or women's suffrage, Paul put into place principles that led to the eventual liberation of both women and slaves. Is the same thing true of homosexuality? Does the trajectory toward greater liberty apply to, say, same-sex marriage within the church or the acceptance of openly gay church members? It is a fair question to ask.

As we have argued in the previous two chapters, we think the best approach to understand how the Bible addresses these issues is proposed by William Webb. Some call his approach the "trajectory hermeneutic."[16] Jesus said the kingdom of God works like yeast in dough (Mt 13:33). At first, it seems a small thing that doesn't appear to be accomplishing anything. You can't see the yeast working, but eventually the effect of the yeast is amazing—the dough rises by two or three times its original volume. Webb argues that sometimes the Bible establishes a principle that initially has little effect but over time produces extraordinary change. But Webb warns that the principle cannot be applied only to issues we like.

There are certain criteria that must be met. For simplicity, he describes the process this way:

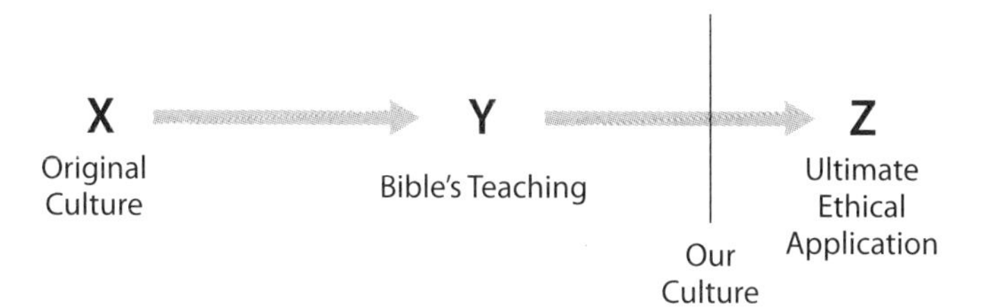

First we determine how the broader culture(s) of Paul's day viewed an issue (X). Then we compare to that perspective the teaching of Paul on the subject. Next we have to ask if Paul's teaching (Y) represents the outer extent of the trajectory, or if God intended the teaching to continue to grow (like yeast). Webb says if Scripture intended us to move beyond "Y," then there will be a "seed" in the text, an idea that moves beyond the "Y" and points toward "Z," the ultimate or ideal ethic.

To review, let's look at how this framework applied in the two previous chapters. In the Greco-Roman world ("X"), women had no rights. They were not allowed (by Romans or Jews) to be educated and thus could not be teachers. They were basically property that a husband or father should take care of but could barter for his advantage. In the New Testament ("Y"), Jesus had women disciples. Paul commends at least one woman as a deaconess (Rom 16:1). The clear trajectory from Paul's culture to Paul's teaching was in the direction of liberating women. Now did Paul describe the full extent of this liberation, or did God intend Paul's teaching to be "yeast" that brought even further change? Paul plants a seed for further growth ("Z"): "There is neither Jew nor Gentile, neither slave nor free, nor is there male and female, for you are all one in Christ Jesus" (Gal 3:28). In this verse, Paul argues that God does not make the same distinctions between his people that the world makes. Status, class, station, gender differences—all are obliterated by the gospel and this is evidenced in the Lord's Supper.

Likewise, Roman culture ("X") taught that it was perfectly normal for some individuals to be the property of others. Seneca argued that slavery was a natural part of the universe. Slaves were property to be bought and sold. The lines between master and slave were clear and distinct. Paul taught ("Y") that slaves and masters were members of the same family; they were Christian brothers and sisters. Paul extends the rights of slaves in a passage that, at first, appears to have nothing to do with slavery:

> For this is the will of God, your sanctification; *that is,* that you abstain from sexual immorality; that each of you know how to possess his own vessel in sanctification and honor, not in lustful passion, like the Gentiles who do not know God; *and* that no man transgress and defraud his brother in the matter. (1 Thess 4:3-6 NASB)

In verse 4 Paul uses a euphemism—"possess his own vessel"—that has two meanings. It can mean to acquire a "vessel" (to get a wife) but it can also mean to control his, *ahem,* "vessel" (to control his genitalia). Paul no doubt intends both applications. One of the reasons Paul gives for controlling the vessel is to avoid the lustful passion of the Gentiles who transgress a brother. To put the matter bluntly, Paul is saying that because the slave is now your brother in Christ, you do not have a right to assault him sexually, no matter what the culture deems appropriate. Instead, the master in this situation should "control his vessel" and "acquire a wife" (or remain faithful to the one he has). Paul's teaching on slavery is moving in a trajectory toward protection and liberation. In fact, the same seed text that applies to women applies to slaves: in Christ, there is neither male nor female, slave nor free, we are all one in Christ Jesus.

Now consider the way the trajectory framework (X → Y → Z) applies to the topic of homosexuality. Roman culture ("X") was very permissive and accepting of homosexual behavior. Although it shamed the passive male, it celebrated the dominant partner in a homosexual relationship. Paul, by contrast, disapproved of both the passive and active partners in homosexual behavior. Paul's teaching ("Y") was more restrictive than the broader culture. There is a trajectory, but instead of moving toward great liberty, it moves toward greater restriction. So this means the trajectory does not work in the same way for homosexuality as it does for women and slaves. So the question we have to ask now is, Is there a "Z," an *even more* restrictive ideal, that Paul advocates for? Should we carry the trajectory further, perhaps excommunicating or even executing, as Leviticus demands, those who practice homosexuality? To take the trajectory further, we need a seed text that carries the idea further.

But there isn't one. As we have already argued, Paul could easily have advocated the Old Testament penalty for homosexuality—exile or execution. He does not. In fact, he clearly identifies the behavior as a sin but includes it among other sins, like gossip. Can we apply Galatians 3:28 (which we used for slaves and women) to homosexuality? No. According to Webb, the seed text has to lie in the same direction as the trajectory from the broader culture to the Scriptural teaching.[17] Paul was arguing for Christians to be more restrictive than their culture on homosexuality. Paul's trajectory on this topic moved in the opposite direction as his teachings on slaves and women. While Paul was moving Christians toward more freedom on the topics of slaves and women, he was moving Christians the opposite direction on the topic of homosexual behavior, towards more restrictions.

Paul on Homosexuality, Slaves, and Women

More restrictive ◄ - - - - - - - - - - - - - - ► Less restrictive

Paul's View on Homosexuality ← Roman Culture → Paul's View on Slavery/Women

Conclusion

Despite the lengthy (and sometimes gritty) explanation to which we've subjected you, we've probably concluded more or less where we began: Paul thinks homosexual behavior is sinful. That's not a position he invented; he retained the prohibition against homosexuality from the Torah. Agree or disagree, Paul's position is unambiguous. What that means practically is that for those who want to follow Paul (as he follows Christ), the challenge is not exegetical but pastoral. To put it another way, the real issue to explore is not what Paul said about homosexuality but how Paul handled folks involved in behaviors with which he disapproved.

There are considerable differences between Paul's first-century context and our own. Many of the sexual behaviors described in this chapter, which then were both legal and socially acceptable (such as pederasty and exploitation of slaves) are neither today. Christians are not divided over these issues. Christians are divided over the question of whether Paul—and God, by extension—might approve of loving, consensual, same-sex relationships between equals. This is a question that Paul would have found difficult, if not altogether impossible, even to comprehend. Roman mores made gay relationships between *equals* virtually impossible.

In the first century, we feel confident Paul would encourage gay Christians to stay single. He encouraged Christians in general to remain single, like he was, and to love folks deeply, like he did. For those burning with sexual desire (whether hetero- or homosexual desire), Paul encouraged heterosexual marriage. We cannot guess if Paul would still give the same pastoral advice in the twenty-first century, but we are certain Paul would not change his theological position about the inappropriateness of homosexuality.

What we do know is this. Regarding the serious issue of sexual morality, Christians in Paul's churches were divided. Many would have balked at the notion that perfectly normal, healthy and socially acceptable gay (and lesbian) sexual relationships were in any way sinful. Many others, in the same congregations, would have been offended, disappointed even, that Paul welcomed into the Christian family those who had engaged in and still were engaging in homosexual behavior. In this way, we find

Immorality in Corinth—a Model for Pastoral Care

If our churches decide to boot out the gays and lesbians, are we prepared to boot out all the other people in sin—the gossips and adulterers and disobedient children? If we argue, "Yeah, but homosexuality is different," we are making a distinction that Paul did not make. Paul grouped people who practiced homosexuality with other sinners: liars, adulterers, rebellious children, slanderers and the arrogant (Rom 1:29-30).

Do we encourage sinfulness? Of course not. We trust Jesus will come to our rescue. The scandal of 1 Corinthians 6 is that after enumerating the list, "men who have sex with men nor thieves nor the greedy nor drunkards nor slanderers nor swindlers will inherit the kingdom of God," Paul adds, "And that is what some of you were" but "you were bought at a price" (1 Cor 6:9-10, 11, 20). That is, the scandal of the gospel is that there is forgiveness and redemption available. We may piously add "even for the vilest offenders," as long as we remember the vilest includes greed, theft and slander, making it hard for any of us to cast the first stone.

ourselves standing where Paul stood. Paul urges people on the one side in the direction of grace. At the same time, he urges people on the other side in the direction of restraint. His goal was not that they meet in the middle in some sort of compromise. Paul's goal was that they will meet in Christian fellowship. He urges them to embrace one another as the Spirit continually conforms them all into the image of Christ as one large family (Rom 8:29), and to be patient with one another as they all strive not to be conformed to the world (Rom 12:2).

In the end, we maintain with Paul that the foundation of Christian community is not perfection or even consensus; it is Christ. Paul insisted that his readers embrace one another as fellow believers before they see eye to eye. The discussion about how to move forward takes place within this community, in which all parties are mutually committed and mutually submitted to one another. We are to love our gay friends as we love our straight friends. Those practicing homosexual behavior belong on the list where Paul put them: with those practicing other sins, such as slandering, lying, drunkenness, gossiping, and with those divorcing and remarrying—a list that includes many in our churches. The scandal of the gospel isn't who it excludes but rather who it includes: Jesus accepts us all. Viewing homosexual behavior in this way places us smack in the middle between our culture and modern Pharisees: a place where Paul often found himself. Jesus accepts gays just like he accepts gossips. He doesn't approve of either behavior, but to both he offers forgiveness and his Holy Spirit.

seven

PAUL WAS A HYPOCRITE

Hypocrites are the worst. Americans cannot abide the politician who denounces commercial-scale animal farming before an urban-elite audience and then praises the practice when he visits the heartland. Our teens scoff at the young person who acts one way around her parents but differently around her friends. (They might do it, but they still view it as wrong.) We crave authenticity and consistency. Many of us would suggest that the basic definition of integrity is that you are the same no matter who you are around. Nobody likes a faker. We are all fairly agreed in denouncing hypocrisy.

That being said, American culture has a fascination with *religious* hypocrites. We disapprove of them, but we find them delicious: the pastor who rails against sexual immorality and is eventually exposed as an adulterer, or the pastor who asks people, in Jesus' name, to sow a seed of faith (i.e., a financial donation) into his ministry and is eventually discovered to be an embezzler. Real-life examples are pervasive enough that the religious hypocrite is practically a stock character in American entertainment.

For this reason, our hypocrisy meter is finely tuned and always pointed in the direction of religious leaders. It would be a crippling indictment if we discovered that Christianity was first propagated by a religious hypocrite. But Femi Aribisala, the fellowship coordinator of the Pentecostal Christian fellowship Healing Wings, argues that it was:

> *No Christian genuinely seeking the righteousness of God should imitate a man like Paul.* Jesus warns his disciples: "Beware of these Pharisees and the way they pretend to be good when they aren't. But such hypocrisy cannot be hidden forever." (Luke 12:1). This warning certainly applies to Paul. Paul declares: "I am a Pharisee, the son of a Pharisee." (Acts 23:6). Moreover, his hypocrisy, hidden in his days, is now evident to all in the Bible. Paul is double-tongued in his epistles. He says one thing here and another thing there. He does the exact opposite of the righteousness he proclaims. The discrepancies between his words and his actions belie his highfalutin pretensions to lofty Christian morality and values.[1]

To boost his argument, Aribisala goes on to call Paul a congenital liar and mean-spirited, an indictment of two different but related charges. Either way, Paul stands accused of an intolerable inconsistency.

Flip-Flopping

On the issue of what to do with a Christian brother or sister who is caught in sin, Paul gives different advice to different churches: he tells the Galatians to "restore" such a sinner "gently" (Gal 6:1), yet he tells the Corinthians to "expel the wicked person from among you" (1 Cor 5:13). Well, which is it? Do you cast him out until he repents or do you keep him in the church and gently disciple him until he sees the error of his ways? Coddle or castigate? Law or grace?

We see the same inconsistency on the issue of food sacrificed to idols. Paul tells one congregation to avoid the meat and another not to worry too much about it. In one chapter, he tells the church in Corinth,

> Some people are still so accustomed to idols that when they eat sacrificial food they think of it as having been sacrificed to a god, and since their conscience is weak, it is defiled. But food does not bring us near to God; we are no worse if we do not eat, and no better if we do. (1 Cor 8:7-8)

Paul suggests it doesn't matter whether or not one eats the food offered to idols. Later in the same letter he tells the same Corinthians, "Do not those who eat the sacrifices participate in the altar? . . . No, but the sacrifices of pagans are offered to demons, not to God, and I do not want you to be participants with demons" (1 Cor 10:18-20). Here he says the food was offered to *demons* and we shouldn't be partners with people who sacrifice to demons. Confusing matters further he tells the Romans, "The one who eats everything must not treat with contempt the one who does not, and the one who does not eat everything must not judge the one who does" (Rom 14:3).

But isn't Paul doing just that? He sure seems to be passing judgment on those who ate the sacrificed food: they were participating with those who sacrifice to demons! So Paul appears to waffle; he's saying different things to different churches. Our grandmothers called this talking out of both sides of his mouth.

Besides his lack of consistency, another (maybe more serious) charge can be raised against Paul. There are times when Paul sounds like an outright hypocrite—he says one thing and *does* another. Four examples come quickly to mind. In 1 Corinthians 6:1 he tells believers they shouldn't appeal to secular courts, although in Acts 25:11 he appeals to the highest secular court on the planet: Caesar himself! Second, Paul's inconsistent attitude about monetary support has been the subject of much study. Paul refuses pay for the gospel (1 Cor 9:1-12). In fact, he is assertive about it:

> If others have this right of support from you, shouldn't we have it all the more?
>
> But we did not use this right. On the contrary, we put up with anything rather than hinder the gospel of Christ. (1 Cor 9:12)

Paul's argument isn't that he didn't need the money, but rather that accepting pay would be a hindrance to the gospel. In fact, Paul brags that he didn't accept financial support from the Thessalonians:

> Surely you remember, brothers and sisters, our toil and hardship; we worked night and day in order not to be a burden to anyone while we preached the gospel of God to you. You are witnesses, and so is God, of how holy, righteous and blameless we were among you who believed. For you know that we dealt with each of you as a father deals with his own children. (1 Thess 2:9-11)

Fathers don't expect their children to pay the bills. Paul lists not accepting money as one of the ways in which he was "holy, righteous and blameless."

This is all well and good, except that Paul *does* accept money from the church in Philippi (Phil 4:15-16) and others (2 Cor 11:8-9). To make the matter worse, *he seems to complain* to the Philippians that no churches would help him financially:

> Moreover, as you Philippians know, in the early days of your acquaintance with the gospel, when I set out from Macedonia, not one church shared with me in the matter of giving and receiving, except you only; for even when I was in Thessalonica, you sent me aid more than once when I was in need. (Phil 4:15-16)

Accepting a gift from other churches but not from the Corinthians offended the Corinthians. Not only does Paul refuse to apologize, he insists he'll keep doing it:

> Was it a sin for me to lower myself in order to elevate you by preaching the gospel of God to you free of charge? I robbed other churches by receiving support from them so as to serve you. And when I was with you and needed something, I was not a burden to anyone, for the brothers who came from Macedonia supplied what I needed. I have kept myself from being a burden to you in any way, and will continue to do so. (2 Cor 11:7-9)

Perhaps more difficult to understand than food and money is that Paul preached consistently throughout his ministry that converts to Christianity shouldn't be circumcised: "Mark my words! I, Paul, tell you that if you let yourselves be circumcised, Christ will be of no value to you at all" (Gal 5:2). Everywhere Paul preached and wrote about circumcision, he delivered this same message without exception. However, Paul demanded that his ministry partner, Timothy, be circumcised before joining him in his missionary efforts. How could he insist Christians in Galatia not allow themselves to be circumcised and then require one of them to be circumcised? Timothy was from Lystra, one of the Galatian churches. Was Christ of no benefit to Timothy? Paul told the Galatians the gospel didn't require circumcision; yet, for Timothy it seems that it did. Paul told a church that if someone preaches a different gospel, let him be damned (Gal 1:8-9). But Paul can't seem to keep his gospels straight.

Finally there is the classic Pauline statement of cultural adaptation that certainly sounds like an endorsement of hypocrisy:

> When I was with the Jews, I lived like a Jew to bring the Jews to Christ. When I was with those who follow the Jewish law, I too lived under that law. Even though I am not subject to the law, I did this so I could bring to Christ those who are under the law. When I am with the Gentiles who do not follow the Jewish law, I too live apart from that law so I can bring them to Christ. (1 Cor 9:20-21 NLT)

Living one way around some people and a different way around others—isn't that the epitome of hypocrisy? And if that's what Paul meant, then he was a hypocrite indeed. Keep in mind, hypocrisy was wrong then and it is wrong now.

In the pages that follow, we consider four main charges: the apostle's teaching and behavior on the issues of meat sacrificed to idols, money, circumcision, and his claim to act differently with Jews and Gentiles.

Meat Sacrificed to Idols

In our church background, Paul's argument about "meat sacrificed to idols" has frequently been commandeered to settle debates about drinking alcohol. Some will argue that the lack of faith of a "weaker brother" shouldn't infringe on their right to enjoy a pint with their buddies. Others will argue that if drinking, however responsibly, causes a brother to "stumble," then we should be happy to be teetotalers. The truth is, in the debate about food sacrificed to idols, Paul's concern had more to do with belief (or superstition) than behavior.

Corinth boasted a meat market built by a generous gift from a wealthy family.[2] The meat at the market was not the problem. Nor was *all* meat a problem. If a Jew wanted chicken for dinner, she could butcher a chicken. If she wanted beef for dinner, theoretically she could butcher a cow. However, where would she find a place to store five hundred pounds of leftover beef in an age before refrigeration? So the practical problem ordinary people faced was where to find one day's worth of meat for the family table. Today, city folks buy meat at the grocery store. Ancient city dwellers did something similar: they went to meat markets to get their hands on a nice steak.

Before it was slaughtered and sold in the market, though, a cow would first be offered to a temple as a sacrifice. A portion of the meat would be kept by the temple to feed its priests and the rest would be returned to the owner. Thus many temples functioned, on a practical level, as butcher shops as well as places of worship. Growing up in Arkansas, when we shot a deer we took it to a "processor." He cut the deer into various fillets, ground some into sausage and otherwise turned the carcass into nicely packaged meat. His fee was a percentage of the meat. Ancient temples operated the same way. We have no way of knowing if the average person took his cow to the temple as an act of worship to his god or goddess or merely to get the meat processed. Perhaps it was a bit of both. The original owner kept however much meat he needed for that day and then sold the rest to the meat market, under the watchful eye of the market officials.

All this is to say that meat sold in a city's meat market was *by definition* meat that had been sacrificed to an idol. There wasn't any way around it. For your typical pagan in Paul's day, this made no difference. In fact it might have been a positive. For a Jew, however, this process posed a serious problem. Meat sacrificed to an idol was unacceptable, as was meat that was processed on the same table as pork or that had, for any number of other reasons, been rendered unclean. Jews living in Nazareth could expect to find kosher meat down at the market, but where would a Jew in Corinth buy kosher meat?

An inscription from the city of Sardis sheds some light. An official decree in Sardis in 47 BC gave Jews various rights and also instructed "the market-officials shall be charged with the duty of having suitable food for them [the Jews] brought in."[3] We have no reason to assume Corinth was any different by Paul's day. Since Gallio had ruled in Corinth that Christians were a subset of Judaism (Acts 18:12-17), market officials would have allowed Christians to buy their meat in a Jewish meat market. Likely for this reason, Paul never addressed the issue while he lived in Corinth. However, when Jews fell out of favor with Emperor Claudius and were expelled from Rome (Acts 18:2), the Jewish meat market in Rome was closed, creating the problem Paul addresses in Romans 14. Some Christians ate the meat from the market while others ate "only vegetables." What happened in Rome trickled out into the Empire. It is easy to imagine that the Jewish meat market in Corinth was also closed sometime after Paul left.[4] That's why he wrote about this problem in his letter to them. What should a Christian do? The only meat available for sale is contaminated by idols. It's possible to become a vegetarian, but some of us would sooner apostatize. Those were pretty much the options.

Paul tells the Corinthians to purchase the meat and to eat it. Ask no questions. There was nothing wrong with the meat: "Eat anything sold in the meat market without raising questions of conscience, for, 'The earth is the Lord's, and everything in it'"

(1 Cor 10:25-26). Christians were not to be troubled that the meat was originally offered to an idol: "As to the eating of food offered to idols, we know that 'no idol in the world really exists'" (1 Cor 8:4 NRSV).

Of course the situation is more complicated than that. Paul notes an exception. What happens when several Christian friends are invited to a banquet, such as the wedding of a co-worker? At the wedding, one Christian might dismiss the source of the meat. Another could be troubled by it—perhaps a Gentile convert who is reminded of offering meat to his former god when he sits at the table. Paul offers this caveat:

> Some people are still so accustomed to idols that when they eat sacrificial food they think of it as having been sacrificed to a god, and since their conscience is weak, it is defiled. . . .
>
> Be careful, however, that the exercise of your rights does not become a stumbling block to the weak. For if someone with a weak conscience sees you, with all your knowledge [that idols are nothing], eating in an idol's temple, won't that person be emboldened to eat what is sacrificed to idols? (1 Cor 8:7-10)

Paul realizes that one Christian had the knowledge that "idols are nothing" and could eat the meat without trouble, but another was still tempted to keep worshiping his former god while also worshiping Christ. He would see the one Christian eating, assume he was worshiping that god, and be emboldened himself to eat the meat as an act of worship to the idol.

This is likely the reason Paul adds a final caution about eating meat. Although he had told his readers to eat the meat without asking questions, he adds, "But if someone says to you, 'This has been offered in sacrifice,' then do not eat it" (1 Cor 10:28).

If Invited, Do I Go?

When Paul was discussing eating meat, he adds, and "you are disposed to go . . ." (1 Cor 10:27 NRSV). This might seem an odd comment. Paul is likely discussing dinner parties where meat was commonly served. But there were other reasons besides idol meat to refuse a dinner invitation: many Roman banquets included "escorts" who provided sexual favors to the guests. This is probably why Paul includes a reference to sexual immorality in his discussion of eating (1 Cor 10:6-13).

The "someone" Paul has in mind is likely the host. If the host notes the meat was sacrificial meat, it is probably an indication that it meant more to the host than mere meat: it was an act of worship to his god, and his guests were invited to join in that act of worship. For Christians who used to worship that god, it was a tempting invitation. Paul warns:

> Therefore, my dear friends, flee from idolatry. . . . Do not those who eat the sacrifices participate in the altar? Do I mean then that food sacrificed to an idol is anything, or that an idol is anything? No, but the sacrifices of pagans are offered to demons, not to God, and I do not want you to be participants with demons. (1 Cor 10:14-20)

When they ate the meat as a sacrifice, they were worshiping the god. Christians were not to join in this worship. In this case, at least, Paul is not being hypocritical or wishy-washy. He is being nuanced. He knows complicated issues such as the consumption of idol meat do not have simplistic answers. It depends on the situation.

ACCEPTING MONEY

Paul unquestionably deals with churches differently with regard to financial support. He accepts gifts from the Philippians and flatly refuses to accept gifts from the Corinthians. Much ink has been spilled on the subject of gift giving.[5] In Paul's world it was a complicated affair because all gifts had strings attached; one gave expecting to receive something back. "When you give or receive, put it all in writing" was ancient Jewish advice (Sir 42:7). You invite those who will invite you back. Reciprocity (giving a gift because you received a gift) was not only expected but considered a virtue in Roman society. In fact, Seneca called it "a sacred bond."[6] Today we say you should give gifts expecting nothing in return. Ancients would have said that's a preposterous idea!

Well, we owe that idea to Jesus:

> Then Jesus said to his host, "When you give a luncheon or dinner, do not invite your friends, your brothers or sisters, your relatives, or your rich neighbors; if you do, they may invite you back and so you will be repaid. (Lk 14:12)

Jesus insisted you should invite the very ones who *can't* reciprocate, but this was a radically new idea for Paul's world and had not yet permeated the Christian church. We assume the Corinthians had not yet gotten the message. (Luke's Gospel hadn't been written yet.) When the Corinthians offered money to Paul they expected him to reciprocate. So if he accepted their gift, Paul would become their "client" and be obligated to do things for them (e.g., if they needed a speaker at an upcoming banquet, he would be expected to come to Corinth). Ancients considered it normal that a patron—the one who gave the gift—should expect special services from the client, somewhat like an employer/employee relationship. Failing to reciprocate to one's patron made one ungrateful—a very serious vice in Paul's world. But Paul had no intention of getting tied to the Corinthians. He had one "patron" to whom he was obligated: Jesus.

The Philippians, by contrast, sent a gift to Paul when he was in prison. Frankly, Paul really needed the gift. Since Roman prisoners had to pay their own costs, Paul could hardly refuse. Yet Paul didn't want to be entangled, and he wasn't able to drop everything and head to Philippi whenever the Philippians had need of him. He needed the gift without the obligations that came with it. By this later point in his ministry, Paul had figured out how to accept the gift in a way that didn't make him their client: Paul spoke of money not as a gift to *him* but as an offering to God (Phil 4:18). The sacred bond the Philippians had secured was between themselves and God. If the Philippians had a need later, they were to look to Paul's God—not to Paul—to meet that need (Phil 4:19).

Getting Paid for Ministry

Paul's approach becomes the model for modern ministers who are paid by the church. A church attender's financial contribution to the church is an offering to God. Although a minister is paid by the church from this offering, the minister is not the church attender's employee, ready at their beck and call. Church members cannot boss around a minister. Ministers are responsible to God, and God provides for them.[7]

The short and long of it is that Paul was not inconsistent about accepting money for ministry. He never accepted money in a way that obligated or entangled him. If the gift had strings attached, Paul refused it. When he could accept a gift in a way that deepened a congregation's connection with God, he jumped at the opportunity.

Circumcision

Acts 15 is the first place we encounter Paul's teaching about circumcision. Some "men from Judea" insisted that in order to be saved, Gentile believers must be circumcised "as required by the law of Moses" (Acts 15:1 NLT). Paul and Barnabas disagreed. They had been evangelizing in Gentile communities and had seen Gentiles convert and embrace the gospel authentically, so they pushed back. They pushed back vigorously and consistently and publicly in Antioch. Eventually after Paul and Barnabas reached an impasse with the other faction, the leaders in Antioch decided to send Paul and Barnabas and some Antiochene representatives down to Jerusalem to discuss this matter with the apostles and the elders. Luke, the writer of Acts, tells us that as they made their way to Jerusalem, the travelers stopped in to visit churches along their route. They were pleased to discover that Gentiles were accepting the faith in all of these churches, but it was precisely these Gentiles that the debate was all about.

When they reach Jerusalem, Paul and Barnabas—and even Peter—testify to their experience of seeing Gentiles embrace faith in Jesus Christ. Not only did these Gentiles receive the faith; they also received the Holy Spirit when they believed. This was Peter's key argument. Gentiles had received the Spirit in the same way as the Jews and had done so without being circumcised. Circumcision was not a prerequisite for the Spirit. And if the Spirit of God accepted the Gentiles just the way they were, then it seemed best to the council in Jerusalem to do the same.

So the council drafted a letter to send home with Paul and Barnabas to the congregation in Antioch explaining that it was the opinion of the apostles and elders in Jerusalem, in keeping with the gospel of Christ, that Gentile believers were not required to be circumcised in order to join the community of faith. In short the council reinforced what Paul and Barnabas had been saying all along.

What's the Big Deal?

The point of all this, of course, is that this discussion about circumcision was a big deal. It was a very big deal, in fact, because it had to do with Christian identity. The council in Jerusalem was the very first ecumenical council of the Christian church. Centuries before other Christian leaders from around the world would meet to debate how Christians should describe and explain the Trinity or the dual natures of Christ, the apostles met to establish a more fundamental issue: What must a Gentile do in order to be accepted as a child of God? Must he or she first become a Jew? Can a person go straight from pagan to saint? Or does she have to pass through the law of Moses first? Although Jewish Christians asked that Gentile Christians not participate in some behaviors that were typically associated with temple worship (Acts 15:29), Paul (and Barnabas) made a principled decision that faith in Christ is the only requirement for salvation, whether for the salvation of Jews or Gentiles.

Paul had stuck to his guns in Antioch, and during his travels down to Jerusalem, and he argued his point passionately before the apostles and elders in Jerusalem. And he was right.

After a weeks-long ordeal, the entire church leadership supported his position. Salvation is by grace alone, through faith, not by works of the law. This decision brought joy to the church (Acts 15:31).

That's probably what you expect from Paul. What you may not expect from Paul is what happens in the very next story in Acts. Just a few short verses after we hear the good news that Gentile converts do not need to be circumcised, Paul sets out on a journey to spread the word. He meets a young man named Timothy, whose mother is Jewish and father is Greek, and asks him to join him on the road. Remarkably, "because of the Jews who lived in that area" where they were traveling, Paul has Timothy circumcised (Acts 16:3). This is a bummer for Timothy who was old enough that he would not soon forget this procedure. Of course, the bigger issue is that Paul's decision in Acts 16 seems to directly contradict his energetic and principled argument. Paul has Timothy circumcised before they "traveled from town to town" to tell other converts that they did not need to be circumcised (Acts 16:4). The passage drips with irony.

While that situation steeps, consider this: Just a few months earlier,[8] Paul had written a letter to Christians in Galatia who had begun to put their hope for salvation in works of the law. The subject of circumcision comes up a lot in Galatians, and Paul has strong words about the issue there. "Mark my words!" he writes, "I, Paul, tell you that if you let yourselves be circumcised, Christ will be of no value to you at all" (Gal 5:2). Back in chapter 2 of the letter, Paul assures the Galatians that the apostles and elders in Jerusalem supported his ministry and his message of salvation by grace (Gal 2:6-10). What's more, he brags that "not even Titus, who was with me, was compelled to be circumcised, even though he was a Greek" (Gal 2:3).

To summarize, Paul was so adamant that Gentile believers should not be circumcised that he fought about it in Antioch, made a special trip to Jerusalem to defend it and spent his career convincing others about it. It makes sense, then, that he would brag about never having Titus circumcised. So how is it not the height of hypocrisy that in the midst of all of this Paul had Timothy circumcised "because of the Jews"?

Context is important. We might be tempted to say that Timothy was half Jewish but ancients viewed ethnicity more like pregnancy: either you were Jewish or you weren't. A generation after Paul, Jewish law officially worked it out: if your mother was Jewish, you were Jewish. We can safely assume that at least some Jews in Paul's day held that view. Thus, to at least some Jews, Timothy was Jewish. But he wasn't circumcised. It's quite possible his Greek father had not permitted it. But in the eyes of Jews, an uncircumcised Jew was one who had willfully *rejected* membership in the Covenant, one who had "cast off the yoke."

Scholars today often say that it was convenient for Timothy to be circumcised in order to join Paul in the synagogue. This is wrong for at least two reasons. First, Gentiles were already allowed in synagogues. Second, we see no hints that Paul did this for "convenience." Circumcising Timothy wasn't a matter of missionary expediency but of cultural communication. Paul didn't want to send the wrong message. Jews seeing Timothy and learning that his mother was Jewish would have assumed that Timothy was one of those Jews who had deliberately forsaken his heritage, who didn't want to be Jewish. Timothy's circumcision or lack thereof would be common knowledge. Public latrines were just a row of seats with no privacy dividers. People relaxed in public baths. There were no toga checks at the synagogue door, but word would have spread that Timothy had not been circumcised. Being with Paul would imply that Paul supported such a view. To the contrary, Paul was proud of his Jewishness:

> For it is we who are the circumcision, we who serve God by his Spirit, who boast in Christ Jesus, and who put no confidence in the flesh—though I myself have reasons for such confidence.
>
> If someone else thinks they have reasons to put confidence in the flesh, I have more: circumcised on the eighth day, of the people of Israel, of the tribe of Benjamin, a Hebrew of Hebrews; in regard to the law, a Pharisee; as for zeal, persecuting the church; as for righteousness based on the law, faultless. (Phil 3:3-6)

Paul expected Jews to be circumcised, whether a Christian or not. Paul noted he was circumcised on the eighth day. Jewish Christians (like other Jews) were circumcised; Gentile Christians (like other Gentiles) were not. Paul refused to have Titus circumcised because to do so would have undermined his theological claim that a Gentile didn't have to become a Jew in order to become a Christian (Gal 2:16). A Gentile *relying* on circumcision (becoming a Jew) for salvation was wrong: "If you are counting on circumcision to make you right with God, then Christ will be of no benefit to you" (Gal 5:2 NLT). With respect to salvation, "circumcision is nothing and uncircumcision is nothing" (1 Cor 7:19). Both Jews and Gentiles can be part of Jesus' kingdom. Nevertheless, a Jew who wasn't circumcised would be seen as one rejecting the yoke of God's covenant. Paul accepted circumcision as a mark of ethnicity but not a means of salvation.

Is Being "All Things to All People" the Height of Hypocrisy?

Did Paul say this to the Corinthians?

> When I was with those who follow the Jewish law, I too lived under that law. . . . When I am with the Gentiles who do not follow the Jewish law, I too live apart from that law. (1 Cor 9:20-21 NLT)

Or did Paul say this?

> When around Jews, I emphasize my Jewishness in order to win them over. . . . *In the same way,* I've made a life outside the law to gather those who live outside the law (although I personally abide by and live under the Anointed One's law). (1 Cor 9:20-21 *The Voice*)

Those are quite different. Both translations are attempting to put what Paul said into modern language, but what we discover is that Paul's actual words were a bit more vague. How you translate them depends upon how you interpret what Paul said.

What Paul actually said was that he became like a Jew to the Jews and like a Gentile to the Gentiles. But what does "became like" mean? We might immediately jump to the assumption Paul was talking about *behavior,* or more specifically behavior related to Torah (Jewish Law). In other words, around sabbath-observing folks Paul observed the sabbath, and around Gentiles who didn't observe the sabbath, Paul didn't either. If that is what Paul meant, he was acting hypocritically. It implies a serpent-like guile. He was misleading Jews into thinking he was Torah observant, when really he wasn't.

But that's not what Paul meant. The best recent research suggests that Paul is not talking about *behavior*; he's talking about rhetorical adaptability, his method of argumentation.[9] Around Gentiles, Paul became "like them" in how he argued his case. When Paul had noted to the Corinthians that some "had knowledge," he argued his case that way, but he didn't adopt the behaviors of the "knowledgeable" (1 Cor 8:1-13). If Paul had been arguing to Jews about meat sacrificed to idols, he would have just quoted Torah. But with the Gentiles in Corinth, Paul used their ways of arguing.

In Acts 17, Luke shows Paul doing this very thing in Athens where Paul argued like a philosopher to win philosophers. When Paul argued, "From one man he made all the nations, that they should inhabit the whole earth" (Acts 17:26), he could easily have quoted Genesis but instead quotes a Greek poet (Acts 17:28). Paul was *rhetorically* adaptive, not *lifestyle* adaptive (which would be duplicitous). So in 1 Corinthians 9, Paul is

Zeus Visits Lystra

The Latin poet Ovid (c. 43 BC–AD 17) records the legend of Zeus visiting the various towns in that region (Phrygia) with his son Hermes, both disguised as ordinary mortals. No one welcomed them. Finally an elderly woodcutter, Baucis, and his wife, Philemon, although quite poor, took them in, offering the last of their food and drink. The food didn't run out and the wine kept welling up, scaring the old couple. When the gods revealed their identity to the old couple, the only reward the couple requested was that they be allowed to be priests to Zeus and die at the same time so that neither would see the tomb of the other. Their request was granted but all the other homes in the region were destroyed.[10]

talking about how one presents the gospel. It depends on the audience. When one talked about God coming to live among us, it meant one thing to Jews who knew the exodus story but another to Gentiles in Lystra. In the exodus, God said he would be our God and we would be his people and he would dwell in our midst (that's the meaning of the Tabernacle). Gentiles in Lystra knew a story where Zeus sneaked down in human disguise to test if folks were hospitable. Paul made the early and painful mistake of using a Jewish argument to a Gentile audience and was stoned over the misunderstanding (Acts 14). Paul learned to argue in Jewish ways to Jews and in Gentile ways to Gentiles.

Paul in Our World

When I was living in Indonesia, our family helper was Muslim. When her child died tragically, we were invited to her home for the funeral. Do we go? "Of course," you might quickly say. But, at the funeral there will be Muslim prayers. Paul's challenges can be ours as well.

Let's bring it closer to home: Your office buddy in the cubicle next to you invites you to her daughter's wedding. Of course you are delighted to go. She is a good friend. She and her husband and you and yours have been to dinner several times. As the date draws near, you get the details. The daughter is getting married at the local temple to Vishnu. You didn't even know there was such a thing in your town. Now what do you do? Paul's advice about idol meat can direct us here. Go, enjoy the wedding (1 Cor 10:25-26). Don't be concerned about the idols in the Hindu temple, for "we know that 'An idol is nothing at all in the world'" (1 Cor. 8:4). If however your buddy considers the wedding to be an act of worship to her god, then Paul would tell us not to go (1 Cor 8:7-10).

Flip-Flopping or Wise Advice?

Let's use a different analogy. Imagine you decide you need to start practicing yoga so you can finally touch your toes. (It's been a long time.) Should you? If you sign up for a course at the local community college and on the first day the instructor says, "Welcome everyone. I'm going to help you relax and get limber," then by all means plunge ahead. Maybe you'll reach those toes one day. If he opens class by saying, "Welcome everyone. I'm going to help you get in touch with Brahman, the all-pervasive energy of the universe," then probably not. You should quietly slip out and not return. If the activity is exercise, there's no harm in it; it will probably do you good. If the activity is intentionally spiritual, a Christian should avoid it; the spiritual world is real, and we shouldn't dabble.

So should Christians practice yoga? "Well," you might conclude, "it depends." Now you sound a lot like Paul. More than that, let's suppose you told a local friend, "Sure, you should take that yoga class. Not an issue," because the yoga class in your city is purely recreational. At the same time, you might have advised a friend in another city that taking a yoga class is a bad idea, because the yoga class in her city, which is much more multicultural, spends a lot of its time talking about chi and the power of universal unity in Brahman. If your friends compare notes, they'll realize that you gave them different advice. Are you talking out of both sides of your mouth? No. Like Paul we learn that complicated issues cannot get simplistic answers. "It depends on the situation" can still be a wise answer.

Once we recognize that pastoral advice often depends on the situation, other situations in which Paul appears inconsistent make sense as well. How does one restore a Christian brother who sins? Well, you might advise one church to restore a brother gently, but advise another church to expel a sinful brother. We are not talking out of both sides of our mouths; we are talking like Paul.

eight

PAUL TWISTED SCRIPTURE

If you were to take an introductory course in biblical interpretation from just about any evangelical college or seminary in the United States, there are a handful of lessons you'd learn everywhere. The first thing you would learn is that the goal of biblical interpretation is to identify the original intent of the biblical author. So instead of asking, What does this mean *to me?* you learn to ask, What did this mean to the *original audience?* The technical term for this is "exegesis." It means to read information *out* (ex-) of the text, instead of reading yourself and your concerns *into* (eis-) the text (that would be "eisegesis").

Then you'll learn some strategies for successful exegesis. One strategy is to read the passage in its historical context because a passage can't mean today what it couldn't have meant back then. To take but one example, in its original historical context Jeremiah 29:11 didn't have anything to do with high school graduates determining the next step of their life journey. Unfortunately, that's how we typically apply the text today: "'For I know the plans I have for you,' declares the Lord, 'plans to prosper you and not to harm you, plans to give you hope and a future.'" The original historical context of this verse was exile; God's people were living as captives in a strange land, but God told them to get comfortable: "Build houses and settle down; plant gardens and eat what they produce. Marry and have sons and daughters; find wives for your sons and give your daughters in marriage, so that they too may have sons and daughters" (Jer 29:5-6). The plans he had for them, the prosperous future he promised, would not be fulfilled for at least a generation. It strains the text to claim that God is here promising you a good job out of college.[1]

Another important strategy is reading a passage within its literary context. If we keep in mind that Exodus 15 is a poem, we can easily imagine this description of the parting of the Red Sea: "By the blast of your nostrils / the waters piled up" (Ex 15:8). We expect colorful imagery in poetry (the literary context), so there's no need to assert that God *literally* parted the Red Sea with a snort or a sneeze.[2]

The final step in the process of interpretation is deciding what a biblical passage means for us today. This is application. Understanding the author's intention and the historical and literary context of a passage creates the parameters within which we determine how the text applies to us today. This is hard work. And it's only after we do this heavy lifting that we can then move on to the equally difficult task of application. We use our best judgment, guided by prayer and reason and the Christian tradition, to determine how to apply what it meant *then* to us *today*. Beginning the process with ground rules doesn't ensure our success, but it disciplines us to hear God speak through the Scriptures, and helps us to avoid hearing our own voice and pretending it was God's. This is pretty basic stuff. Bible Interpretation 101.

PAUL, EVANGELICALS AND SCRIPTURE

The typical evangelical approach to biblical interpretation, which we've been describing, is a form of the historical-critical method. We use it for very important reasons. To begin with, we believe the Bible is entirely true and authoritative and that it has something important and relevant to say to us. We also are keenly aware of how Christians throughout the ages have mishandled the Bible. Remember that Christian slaveholders in the antebellum South appealed to the Bible to justify owning slaves, and Martin Luther quoted the Bible to buttress the dreadful anti-Semitism of his old age. Armed with a responsible methodology, we hope to protect ourselves from making these sorts of errors. Your authors were both taught these principles in seminary, and we both teach them to aspiring young exegetes. The thing is, the more time we spend reading the letters of Paul, the clearer it becomes that Paul didn't follow the rules we teach.

Believe it or not, the apostle Paul violates just about all of our historical-critical principles when he interprets the Old Testament in his letters. Usually he breaks one rule or another; rarely does he violate all of them at once, but sometimes he does even that.

Romans 9:25 is a helpful example. Paul is wrapping up an argument about how God has intended from the beginning to include Gentiles in his plan of salvation. He quotes the prophet Hosea, "I will say to those called 'Not my people,' 'You are my people'; and they will say, 'You are my God'" (Hos 2:23). The people who are "not my people" Paul identifies as Gentiles. The problem is, this can't be what Hosea meant.

In the *historical* context of Hosea's prophecy, the people of Israel are in exile. Because Israel was far from God (spiritually) and far from the Promised Land (geographically), it was as if they were no longer God's people. Furthermore, God had warned his people (the Israelites) that if they broke his covenant, he would declare them "not my people" (Hos 1:8-9).

The *literary* context of the passage confirms "You are not my people" is a poetic name for Israel (Hos 1:10). Using our contemporary historical-critical method, the only possible interpretation of Hosea's prophecy is that one day God will restore his beloved people, the nation of Israel. Clearly Hosea was *intending* to talk about God restoring the people of Israel. Thus Paul ignores the principle of authorial intention and interprets the passage in a way that Hosea never intended. He takes it to mean that one day Gentiles will be accepted into God's family. Paul tramples the rules of Bible Interpretation 101.

This is standard practice for Paul. Leroy Huizenga has admitted that if Paul had been a student in his introductory hermeneutics course, Paul would have failed. He calls out Paul's allegorizing in Galatians 4 (which we'll talk about more later) as a particular offense:

> The textbook example of hermeneutical jujitsu, however, is Paul's brazen *tour de force* in Galatians 4:21-31, in which he states that Hagar and Sarah are allegories (*allēgoroumena*), the former pointing to the slavery of the Judaizers of the earthly Jerusalem and the latter pointing to the freedom of the heavenly Jerusalem. Perhaps that might fly in homiletics, but not in serious exegesis. If one were to hand out grades, it would be F's all around.[3]

Paul's approach to interpreting the Bible is different enough from modern methods that one Bible scholar has concluded, "The way Paul handled his Bible—what we call the Old Testament—would keep him off the short list for openings to teach Bible in many

Evangelical seminaries and Christian colleges."[4] That's right: Paul, the author of most of our New Testament, wouldn't be allowed to teach a course on how to interpret Scriptures.

PAUL'S APPROACH TO THE BIBLE

Let us be clear. The apostle Paul believed that the Bible was divinely inspired by God, that the entire truth of God was contained in the Scriptures and that the reason God gave his people the Bible is so we would know how to live faithfully today—in whatever age "today" might be. So far, this is really good news. We can confidently say that Paul shared with modern evangelicals basically the same convictions about the Bible. It's in the nuts and bolts of how Paul does exegesis that things begin to look a little strange.

In Romans 9, for example, Paul defends the justice of God for choosing to accept his children on the basis of faith, not works. In the process, he pulls in quotations from Genesis, Exodus, Malachi, Hosea and Isaiah. He argues that not all descendants of Abraham are included in God's promises, but only those descended through Isaac (Gen 18:10, 14; 21:12; 25:23). He argues this decision is in keeping with God's sovereign justice (Ex 9:16; 33:19). He argues that this decision is what enables Gentiles to be included in God's salvation, for his glory (Hos 1:10; 2:23), and that this all fulfills the prophecy that not all of Israel will be saved (Is 1:9) because many will stumble over the teaching that they are saved by faith and not by works (Is 8:14; 28:16). These quotations, which Paul stitches seamlessly together, are written by different authors with different intents, to different audiences at different times in history and in different genres of literature.

This is what modern readers would call prooftexting: the practice of pulling quotations out of context, and sometimes thrusting unrelated quotations together, in order to justify a position that the quotations wouldn't necessarily defend in their original context. This can seem relatively harmless if we pull together Exodus 1:7 ("The Israelites were exceedingly fruitful; they multiplied greatly, increased in numbers and became so numerous that the land was filled with them") and Luke 10:37 ("Go and do likewise."). However, the potential for abuse is apparent if we pull together Matthew 27:5 ("So Judas threw the money into the temple and left. Then he went away and hanged himself") with Luke 10:37 ("Go and do likewise"). Prooftexting violates the principles of authorial intention, historical and literary context, and saving application until after interpretation.

Prooftexting a Warning?

In 2 Corinthians 6:14-18, Paul strings together verses from Leviticus, 2 Samuel, Isaiah, Jeremiah and Ezekiel, even sticking some verses into the middle of others. Some of the verses were talking about the exodus, some about returning from the exile (that's two different historical contexts) and some were warning those who carry sacred instruments for the temple not to touch unclean things (a very specific literary context). Paul uses all of them to warn Christians not to partner with (including marry) non-Christians: "Do not be yoked together with unbelievers" (2 Cor 6:14).

Paul: A Pharisee of Pharisees

Paul interpreted the Bible the way he did because he wasn't a twenty-first-century evangelical Christian in the global West. He was a Jew and, more specifically, a highly trained Pharisee.

He was "a Pharisee, descended from Pharisees" (Acts 23:6) who was "thoroughly trained in the law of our ancestors" (Acts 22:3). Learned Jewish exegetes had developed a thorough method of biblical interpretation before Paul's generation. The exegetical method that predominated in Paul's day was codified by the famous Jewish exegete, Hillel. Paul was mentored by a rabbi named Gamaliel (Acts 22:3), who was the grandson of Hillel. Scholars generally agree that Paul interpreted the Old Testament the way other Pharisees of his day interpreted the Old Testament. And, actually, that would make sense.

Paul inherited a full toolkit of exegetical methods from this tradition, including midrash, literalism, pesher and allegory. Modern students of Scripture are told to stay a long way from these methods. Pesher and allegory are considered anathema in most college Bible classes. We do not merely avoid them, as if they have fallen out of fashion. We warn students to stay far from them. Let's look at a few of Paul's interpretive methods.

Midrash. The goal of midrash was rock solid: it was an effort to apply God's word "back then" to hearers "today." But it wasn't simply a matter of application. Midrash was a creative, even imaginative, engagement with a difficult or confusing passage with the goal of revealing the passage's relevance to the contemporary reader. The term may be unfamiliar, but Christians who attend church regularly will be familiar with the concept. We hear a midrash on Scripture most Sundays when a pastor seeks to apply a particular passage to our lives today. When pastors talk about the "eternal truth" of a passage or a "timeless biblical principle," they are often doing midrash. It's an effort to show how the word of God in the past is still just as applicable in the present.

While the *goal* of midrash is the same today, the *method* isn't. Paul's teacher taught seven rules for interpreting Scripture (we'll look at some of them later). There is nothing inherently wrong with the concept of midrash, but in Paul's day, it often used methods that violate our modern rules of exegesis. When Paul does midrash in Romans 9, he is not as concerned about the original context or meaning of Hosea as he is about how the story of Hosea *applies* to readers in Paul's own day and time. Using midrash, Paul shifts the focus from what "my people" meant *back then* to what it means *today*, that everyone by faith may be called God's people. Midrash wasn't done in a willy-nilly or arbitrary way, as we'll see in a bit.

Literalism. Literalism is assuming that Scripture means what it literally says. Growing up, we remember bumper stickers that asserted, "God said it. I believe it. That settles it." We appreciate the sentiment. At first glance, it seems pious to say Scripture is literally true. Yet if that's true, what do we do with verses like, "the mountains leaped like rams, the hills like lambs" (Ps 114:4)? We quickly reply that it is a psalm, a poem/song. The Bible isn't teaching that mountains actually leaped like a ram. In other words, we shouldn't take *that* verse literally. But then how do we know which passages to take literally? What do we do with Jesus' command?

> If your hand or your foot causes you to stumble, cut it off and throw it away. It is better for you to enter life maimed or crippled than to have two hands or two feet and be thrown into eternal fire. And if your eye causes you to stumble, gouge it out and throw it away. It is better for you to enter life with one eye than to have two eyes and be thrown into the fire of hell. (Mt 18:8-9)

Even if our hearts are in the right place, literalism can often get us into trouble. If our hearts are in the wrong place, literalism can be a tool to get us out of discipleship. Leviticus tells us to "love your neighbor as yourself" (Lev 19:18). Literalists in Jesus' day wanted to know who was *literally* my neighbor. The fellow next door? What about the guy who lives two houses down? They wanted to use a literalistic interpretation to draw boundaries that delineated clearly how far they needed to love. The Mishnah, a rabbinical text codified during the first and second centuries, used a literal interpretation of Deuteronomy 21:18-21 to indicate all the conditions that would exclude a son from being declared a "stubborn and rebellious son":

> If one of them [his father or his mother] had a hand or fingers cut off, or was lame, dumb, blind or deaf, he does not become a "stubborn and rebellious son," because it is written, "then shall his father and his mother lay hold on him"—this excludes those with hand or fingers cut off, "and bring him out," excluding the blind, "he will not obey our voice," excluding the deaf. (*Mishna Sanhedrin* 71a.)

Paul sometimes seized on the literalistic interpretation of a word or phrase when the situation called for it. In Galatians 3:16 he quotes one of the many references in Genesis to the seed of Abraham. In Hebrew, the word "seed" is a "generic singular" (like the words "sheep" or "deer"), referring to all of Abraham's descendants (cf. Gen. 12:7; 13:15; 15:18; 17:7-8; 22:17-18; 24:7).[5] Paul argues that since it *literally* says "seed" (singular) and not "seeds" (plural), then it is referring to one person and that person is Christ. Furthermore, in the context of Genesis, the singular "seed" should be Isaac, not Jesus. Here Paul's interpretation is literalistic as it regards grammar but not as it regards the literary context.

Pesher. Hebrew for "solution" or "interpretation," pesher presupposes every text has two meanings. The surface-level meaning is there for normal, uneducated people. Beneath this superficial meaning is a hidden or secret interpretation accessible only to specially trained experts. A pesher interpretation requires an additional ingredient: an eschatological worldview. That is, pesher presupposes that a particular prophetic message from past ages was actually being fulfilled in the reader's lifetime. The deeper, spiritual interpretation of a text was a mystery until that moment in history. In the reader's day, the mystery was now plain to those with eyes to see (and an expert to explain it). Pesher tries to connect a contemporary situation directly to the ancient text. In Paul's day the contemporary enemy, Rome, was connected directly to Habakkuk's text. This interpretive approach experienced something of a revival in the 1970s through the 1990s. On a shelf in my office, I (Brandon) have an end times prophecy decoder. Next to literal descriptions from the book of Revelation (text) are spiritual interpretations (pesher) of what those people or objects represent. Beside the description "armored locusts" of Revelation 9:1-10, the decoder explains the modern reader should interpret, "Russian military helicopters."

Does Paul use pesher? Many scholars answer yes.[6] Take for example Paul's teaching in 2 Corinthians 3:7-18 when he uses the story of Moses covering his face with a veil after talking with God (Ex 34:29-35). Paul appears to say the veil is referring to Jews in his day reading the Old Testament and not understanding its true meaning: "Even to this day when Moses is read, a veil covers their hearts. But whenever anyone turns to the Lord, the veil is taken away" (2 Cor 3:15-16). The story of Moses' veil wasn't a historical detail, Paul tells us, but actually a spiritual mystery that no one really understood until Paul's moment in time. Now the real meaning is plain: there was no real unveiling of Scripture until Christ came.

Allegory. Pesher is unusual, but the interpretive method Paul uses that often makes evangelical readers most uncomfortable is his use of allegory. Allegories looked for the deeper "spiritual" meaning behind what appeared to be a simple story. Jews had a story that the rock Moses struck to provide water (Num 20:11) became a well that followed the Israelites through the wilderness.[7] Paul accepts this traditional story and then allegorizes it, identifying the rock/well as Christ (1 Cor 10:4).

A Christian Allegory of the Good Samaritan

The church father Augustine famously allegorized Jesus' parable reinterpreting these elements:

Element in Jesus' Parable	The "Spiritual Meaning"
The man going down to Jericho	Adam
Jerusalem (from where he left)	The City of Heavenly Peace
Jericho (where he was heading)	Mortality
The robbers	The devil and his angels
Stripping him	Taking away his immortality
Beating him	Persuading him to sin
Leaving him half dead	Spiritually dead although physically alive
The priest	The Law
The Levite	The Prophets
The Good Samaritan	Christ (of course)
Binding the wounds	Restraint of sin
Oil	The comfort of hope
Wine	The exhortation to work
The inn	The church
The Innkeeper	The apostle Paul
The promised return	The resurrection of Christ

Distilled from Robert H. Stein, *The Method and Message of Jesus' Teachings*, rev. ed. (Louisville: WJK, 1994), 46.

Galatians 4 contains the clearest and most complex allegory in the New Testament. Paul's main goal in Galatians is to explain why Gentile Christians are not second-rate members of God's household, even though they joined the family late. They are full members. The keystone quotation in his letter to the Galatians, the passage that pulls the argument together, is an appeal to the story of Sarah (the wife of Abraham) and Hagar (Sarah's slave) and their children. We quote Paul at length (because this passage is often skipped over by evangelical readers):

> Tell me, you who want to be under the law, are you not aware of what the law says? For it is written that Abraham had two sons, one by the slave woman and the other by the free woman. His son by the slave woman was born according to the flesh, but his son by the free woman was born as the result of a divine promise.
>
> These things are being taken figuratively [*allēgoroumena,* allegorically]: The women represent two covenants. One covenant is from Mount Sinai and bears children who are to be slaves: This is Hagar. Now Hagar stands for Mount Sinai in Arabia and corresponds to the present city of Jerusalem, because she is in slavery with her children. But the Jerusalem that is above is free, and she is our mother. For it is written:
>
> "Be glad, barren woman,
> you who never bore a child;
> shout for joy and cry aloud,
> you who were never in labor;
> because more are the children of the desolate woman
> than of her who has a husband." (Gal 4:21-27)

Paul concludes that the Gentiles, like Isaac, are "children of promise" (Gal 4:28), even though they are not Abraham's offspring biologically. That means Jews and Gentiles, by faith, stand equal before God. Paul uses allegory to get at the deeper spiritual meaning beneath the literal meaning of the story of Abraham's two sons.

PAUL'S APPROACH IN CONTEXT

So was Paul just playing fast and loose with the text? Was he twisting it to fit his purposes, making it say whatever he wanted it to say? Was Paul breaking the rules back then too?

Since Paul was trained by the grandson of Hillel, we are not surprised to find Paul using at least some of Hillel's rules for interpreting Scripture. Hillel's second rule argued for "stringing pearls." This refers to the practice of gathering passages from several places in the Bible. If a particular word is found in two different passages, the verses will be connected in order to support an argument, regardless of the original context of either verse. A particular word ("pearl") found in one verse and then in another verse is used to connect (string) the verses together. For example, the Babylonian Talmud (a collection of Jewish oral teachings on Scripture) records:

> The All-Merciful ordained, "thou shalt not oppress thy neighbor nor *rob* him" [Lev. 19:13], and then directs that, "he shall restore that which he took by *rob*bery" [Lev. 5:23]; then again . . . the All-Merciful ordained, "thou shalt not go into his house to fetch [take, *rob*] his *pledge*" [Deut. 24:10-13], and then, "thou shalt stand without . . . thou shalt surely restore to him the *pledge* when the sun goes down" [Deut. 24:19-21].[8]

The rabbi used various forms of the word "rob" to connect three verses. Then a second word in the last verse is used to build a second layer, stringing the pearl, "pledge." In the New Testament, the best example of stringing pearls is the Letter to the Hebrews.[9]

But Paul does it too. When critiquing those in Corinth who considered themselves "wise" (*soph-*), Paul strings two verses using "wise," one from Job 5:13 and the other from Psalm 94:11.

> For the wisdom [*soph-*] of this world is foolishness in God's sight. As it is written: "He catches the wise [*soph-*] in their craftiness" [Job 5:13]; and again, "The Lord knows that the thoughts of the wise [*soph-*] are futile" [Ps 94:11]. (1 Cor 3:19-20)

Paul tells the Corinthians they will experience "not-death" (*a-thanat-*) and then strings verses from Isaiah and Hosea using the pearl "death" (*thanat-*).

> When the perishable has been clothed with the imperishable, and the mortal [*thnāt-*] with immortality [*a-thanat-*], then the saying that is written will come true: "Death [*thanat-*] has been swallowed up in victory [Is 25:8]."
>
> "Where, O death [*thanat-*], is your victory?
> Where, O death [*thanat-*], is your sting? [Hos 13:14]"
> (1 Cor 15:54-55)

He strings together two verses from Hosea using "not my people" in Romans 9:25-26, the pearl "stone" (*lithos*) in Romans 9:33, and so on. While we might note that the original context of each Old Testament quotation seems trampled on—an important consideration in *our* day—Paul is following the interpretive rules of *his* day.

Hillel argued that one could reason from a "light" example to a "heavy" one. Both Jesus and Paul used this technique, often marked in English translations by the phrase "how much more?" Thus, Jesus teaches that since God cared to clothe the grass of the field, *how much more* will God clothe you (Mt 6:30)? If we being evil fathers still give good gifts to our children, *how much more* will our heavenly Father give to us (Mt 7:11)? Likewise, Paul argues that since we will judge angels, *how much more* the things of this life (1 Cor 6:3)? If the ministry of Moses was glorious, causing his face to shine, *how much more* glorious will be our ministry (2 Cor 3:7-11)?

Hillel argued you can move from general to particular or vice versa. When Paul discusses love in Romans 13, he cites several particular commandments from Exodus 20: don't commit adultery, don't murder, don't steal, don't covet. He concludes that "Love your neighbor as yourself" (Lev 19:18) is the general commandment that summarizes the particulars (Rom 13:9).

Allow us one more rule of Hillel where a similar idea "found in another place" can be brought in. This rule was often used to resolve what seemed to be conflict between two stories by referring to a third. In Leviticus 1:1, God meets with his people *in the tent of meeting*. In Exodus 25:22, he meets with them *above the Ark of the Covenant*. A rabbi resolved this apparent contradiction by appealing to Numbers 7:89: "When Moses entered the *tent of meeting* to speak with the LORD, he heard the voice speaking to him from between the two cherubim *above the atonement cover on the ark of the covenant law*" (emphasis added). This resolves the apparent discrepancy by combining the two descriptions.

In a more creative instance, a tradition developed to resolve what someone deemed a conflict. In Exodus 19:20, God came down to Mount Sinai but in Exodus 20:19-22, God spoke out of heaven. So tradition states that God brought the heavens down to Mount Sinai and then spoke to Moses (*m. Sifra* 1:7).

With all that in mind, let's look at an example where *at first glance* it might look like Paul was twisting Scripture. In

Galatians 3, Paul begins citing Genesis 15:6 that *Abraham believed* and was declared righteous. He strings a couple of pearls related to the root word for "believe." He strings the pearl that Abraham *believed* (*pist-*) to his statement "those who have *faith* (*pist-*) are children of *Abraham*," and argues from a particular (Abraham who had faith) to a general (all those who have faith). He then uses analogy to connect this idea to Genesis 12:3, "All peoples on earth will be blessed through you [Abraham]." He then connects blessing with curses and strings pearls from several passages about curses together, ending with "Anyone who is hung on a pole is under God's curse" (Deut 21:23), connecting the general (anyone hung on a pole) to a particular (Jesus) to say that Jesus bore the curse for us (Gal 3:10-14). Whew! But Paul isn't done. He then uses Hillel's rule to bring "from another place" a reference to Abraham in Genesis 12:7:

> The promises were spoken to Abraham and to his seed. Scripture does not say "and to seeds," meaning many people, but "and to your seed," meaning one person, who is Christ. (Gal 3:16)

Paul concludes by using literalism, emphasizing "seed" was singular. Even though we might struggle to keep up with Paul here, keep in mind that this exegesis conformed to the established and accepted rules of his day.

Likewise, it appears at first glance that Paul merely uses pesher to say that Moses' veil really refers to Paul's contemporary situation where Jews did not correctly understand the Old Testament. A more careful study has shown, though, that Paul is actually drawing from a long Jewish tradition connecting Moses with "glory" (*doxa*).[10] Paul then uses the acceptable methods of his day in his application. Although our heads are spinning, his

Jewish Christian readers would have been nodding their heads, with a knowing "mm-hmm."

So, Are We Misreading Scripture?

Readers of Paul haven't always considered his exegetical methods strange or suspicious. Very early on, Christians tried to imitate Paul's interpretive practices themselves and, with some adjustments, the use of midrash, stringing pearls, pesher and allegory were pretty standard tools in Christian exegetical and theological work until just a couple hundred years ago. Origen, a highly influential theologian from the third century, considered Paul's way of reading Scripture to be essential to his ministry to Gentiles. "The apostle Paul," Origen wrote, "taught the Church which he gathered from the Gentiles how it ought to interpret the books of the Law. These books were . . . formerly unknown to the Gentiles and were very strange." Origen believed the Jews had misunderstood the Bible and that's why they rejected Christ.[11] Origen thought Paul made some necessary adjustments to Jewish interpretive method, changes that made it clear that the Scriptures pointed to Jesus. Thus Origen thought it was important to imitate Paul's exegesis. It was Paul's method, a method Origen considered uniquely Christian, that prevented the error of unbelief. He wanted to read the Bible faithfully as a Christian, taking seriously the example of Paul.

Origen certainly practiced what he preached. At times he spiritualized even the most literal of passages. When the Bible reports in Exodus 12 that the Israelites left Egypt and journeyed from Rameses to Sukkoth (Ex 12:37), it is giving us a map of their journey. Origen strings pearls from both the Old Testament and the New Testament and allegorizes each element. Thus, "Rameses" means "the commotion of a *moth*," Origen explains, and Jesus tells us not to store *treasure* where the *moth* destroys (Mt 6:20); instead, your *treasure* will be in heaven if you sell all your possessions and follow Christ (Mt 19:21). So, Origen concludes, the spiritual meaning of the Israelites' journey from Rameses to Sukkoth is that we should leave all we have behind and follow Christ.

This is an interpretation most of us would reject today. But Origen claimed his method was an effort to stay true to Paul's approach to the Bible.

> What then are we to do who received such instructions about interpretation from Paul, a teacher of the Church? Does it not seem right that we apply this kind of rule which was delivered to us in a similar way in other passages? . . . It seems to me that if I differ from Paul in these matters I aid the enemies of Christ. . . . Let us cultivate, therefore, the seeds of spiritual understanding received from the blessed apostle Paul, in so far as the Lord shall see fit to illuminate us by your prayers.[12]

So if Paul interpreted Scripture one way and we go about it a different way, doesn't that mean one of us does it right and one of us does it wrong? If we avoid allegorical interpretations, are we aiding the enemies of Christ, as Origen warned? Thankfully, no. At the end of the day, the disagreement between Paul's method and our own isn't truly that pronounced. We've pointed out in this chapter even the most unusual (by contemporary standards) examples of Paul's exegetical method were following the rules of his day. Nonetheless, the truth is, in the majority of places, Paul interpreted the Old Testament much as we do. For most of Paul's exegesis, we are not that far apart.

In fact, since the Reformation, Protestants have considered it more faithful to Paul's example (and to the Bible in general) to look for the "natural and simple" meaning of Scripture. In his commentary on Galatians, John Calvin insisted that allegory and literalism, for example, are not mutually exclusive approaches to the text. Calvin explains Paul "certainly did not mean that Moses wrote the story [about Abraham, Sarah and Hagar] with the intention that it should be used as an allegory. What he [Paul] is saying is that there is a relevance in the story to the present case. His comparison does not deny the literal meaning of the original text . . . [and] it did not involve a departure from the literal sense of the text."[13]

What set Paul, and the other earliest believers, apart was his assumption that Jesus Christ was the long-awaited Messiah, as the resurrection proved. He didn't need to learn from the Scriptures that Jesus had risen. He met the risen Lord on the road to Damascus. Because he was convinced that Jesus was the one prophesied about in the Scriptures, he read all of the Scriptures as fulfilled in Christ. Indeed, his interpretation of the Scriptures was radically Christocentric; Paul presupposed that all Scripture was fulfilled in Christ. Jesus is the key that unlocks the meaning of Israel's Scriptures. Yes, Hosea was talking about the restoration of God's people. In retrospect or, better, when viewed through Christ, we know that God's people include Gentiles who believe. So Paul knew Hosea's original meaning, but Paul refused to read and interpret it apart from Christ. Those "who were not my people" are now "my people," ultimately and entirely, in Jesus. For Paul, Scripture had been pointing in this direction from the beginning. Pesher requires the interpreter to believe that his contemporary time was the prophesied end of time. Paul (and other New Testament writers) believed it was, that Jesus inaugurated the end times. Prophecies about the "Day of the Lord" really *were* about

Jesus. Thus, Peter believed that Pentecost was the fulfillment of Old Testament prophecy:

> This is what was spoken by the prophet Joel:
> 'In the last days, God says,
> I will pour out my Spirit on all people.'" (Acts 2:16-17)

For Paul, the Old Testament "Day of the Lord" was the "Day of the Lord Jesus" (2 Cor 1:14). It isn't twisting Scripture if it is true.

Reading Deeply with Paul

Paul wasn't twisting Scripture; he was doing exegesis according to the rules of his day. He was behaving badly in the sense that he considered Christ the key to unlocking the deeper spiritual meaning of the Bible. While his contemporaries would have agreed that there *was* a deeper spiritual meaning in Scripture, they would not have agreed that Christ was the key to unlocking it. Beyond that, Paul used arguments that his readers (and his opponents) would accept as valid ways to read Scripture, deftly arguing that Jesus was the promised Messiah.

Sometimes Paul is accused of pulling a verse out of context when in reality he is making a profound theological statement. For example, Paul quotes Joel 2:32, which refers to Yahweh (the LORD), and applies it to Jesus in Romans 10:13: "Everyone who calls on the name of the Lord will be saved." Actually he does this a lot (Jer 9:24 in 1 Cor 1:31; Is 40:13 in 1 Cor 2:16; Ps 24:1 in 1 Cor 10:26 and many more). Paul isn't playing loose with the context. Rather, he is insisting that Jesus *is* Yahweh, the God of the Old Testament. Scholars call this "Yahweh Christology."[14] What at first glance seems trampling context was actually deep theologizing. Paul is not confused. He is making a powerful point, the same point John made in John 1:1 and that Jesus made when he referred to himself as "I am" (Jn 8:58).

We began by noting Paul's apparent misquoting of Hosea's passage about "not my people." Hosea reasoned that Israel had broken her covenant with God (through Moses). God had warned if Israel did not keep her part of the covenant, they would no longer be his people and they would lose the land. And so it happened. After the destruction of the temple and the loss of the land, what then? God promised through Jeremiah,

> They shall be My people, and I will be their God. . . . I will make an everlasting covenant with them that I will not turn away from them, to do them good; and I will put the fear of Me in their hearts so that they will not turn away from Me. (Jer 32:38-40, NASB)

Many are familiar with his promise:

> "The days are coming," declares the LORD,
> "when I will make a new covenant
> with the people of Israel
> and with the people of Judah." (Jer 31:31)

Paul was familiar with Jesus' use of "new covenant." He quotes Jesus (1 Cor 11:25), but more than that, Paul considered himself a servant of the new covenant (2 Cor 3:6). And Paul considered Gentiles to be full members of the new covenant. Therefore, we have to conclude that Paul wasn't really pulling Hosea out of context. Rather, Paul was weaving an argument that God is making a new people, a new Israel that would include Gentiles grafted into the tree of Israel (Rom 11:17). He demonstrates that the context is much broader and more profound than God's people, including the prophets, had yet imagined. And in proving his point, Paul skipped over all the steps in the argument, jumping straight to the conclusion that Gentiles are now also sons of the living God (Rom 9:26). This isn't the only time Paul seems to draw odd conclusions from Scripture when really he is jumping over the steps in an argument. Paul assumes his more sophisticated readers will follow his exegetical argument.

Sometimes we sell Paul and his audience short. As moderns, we may assume ancient readers were not as sophisticated as we are. Or to put it more bluntly, we assume we are smarter. C. S. Lewis called this chronological snobbery. While we may have smartphones and Bible software, we are probably no smarter. In fact, it's quite possible at least some of Paul's readers were more sophisticated readers than we are, having memorized large portions of Scripture. We should not assume Paul's readers were incapable of following a complex rhetorical argument, just because we have trouble following it.

So we have to conclude a couple of things about Paul's use of Scripture. First, he often is making a more complex argument than we may realize at first blush. He isn't pulling out of context or twisting Scripture; rather he is weaving a nuanced point. Second, Paul has different exegetical rules. He uses the rules of his day. It isn't fair to fault him for not using ours. He reaches correct conclusions using the interpretive methods his readers knew and accepted. We have rules we consider better today, largely because they are less easily abused.

A key difference between Paul's approach to the Bible and ours is that he had a few more tools in his tool chest than we allow ourselves today. In addition to the literal reading, Paul used midrash. We use a version of midrash today via the historical-critical method. Yet Paul also employed pesher and allegory (and typology, the use of recurring patterns). These are tools for the advanced reader of the Bible. When new exegetes are taught to interpret Scripture, we take allegory, pesher and typology off the table and teach exclusively the historical-critical method. We do this because this method is safe and reliable. It keeps us within the boundaries of orthodoxy with greater frequency. When everyone is following the same rules, we have

Smartphones Might Not Make Us Smarter

Since we can easily look things up, we today often have less information memorized. Alas, we may be proof of the very claim Plato made condemning the art of writing. About four hundred years before Paul, Plato tells the (fictitious) story of the minor Egyptian god Theuth who presented to the head god Thamus (roughly the Egyptian equivalent of Zeus) the invention of writing, claiming, "'This invention, O king,' said Theuth, 'will make the Egyptians wiser and will improve their memories' (274)." But Thamus replies,

> Now you, who are the father of letters, have been led by your affection to ascribe to them a power the opposite of that which they really possess. For this invention will produce forgetfulness in the minds of those who learn to use it, because they will not practise [*sic*] their memory. Their trust in writing . . . will discourage the use of their own memory . . . You offer your pupils the appearance of wisdom, not true wisdom, for they . . . will therefore seem to know many things, when they are for the most part ignorant.[15]

Likewise today, because someone can quickly google a fact or "search" for information on our phones, we can think that we are knowledgeable. But when everything is at our fingertips, it seems less is etched on our hearts and minds.

checks and balances by which other exegetes can verify or challenge our results. Essentially, our modern approach minimizes human interpretive error. For these reasons, it is a great method for rightly interpreting the Word of God and hearing from him in Scripture.

The historical-critical method is a great way to achieve these things, but it is not the only way. When we take tools like allegory, pesher and typology off the table, we do so temporarily. Over time, we must add them back.[16] (Pesher should probably stay off the table, since how would we know that this year is the year for the second coming?) Because allegory and typology are easily misused, they are only safe in the hands of seasoned and experienced exegetes.

When we say "seasoned and experienced exegetes," we don't mean people with Bible degrees. This is not a case of educational snobbery. There have been plenty of illiterate, uneducated Christians throughout the ages who knew the Scriptures deeply and intimately and could exegete circles around the two of us. Neither of my (Brandon's) grandmothers have any formal education in hermeneutics, but both are so steeped in the Scriptures that they can follow Paul's subtle connections, inductive reasoning and literary allusions. His words, *the* Word, is *in* them. I (Randy) taught an in-depth Bible study at my church for years. The class was made up mostly of Bible majors and seminary students. But there were also what I call "Sunday School veterans," including three Jamaican widows who sat near the back of the room. They had grade-school educations, but these grandmothers knew—I mean really *knew*—their Bible. In one class, I was teaching Galatians and had reached Paul's claim of being called in his mother's womb (Gal 1:15). One of the grandmothers raised her hand and asked, "Is this like when God called Jeremiah to be a prophet?" She was way ahead of me. "Yes," I said, "this was typology. Paul was trying to remind us of someone else." I was greeted by a sea of blank looks elsewhere. I added, "Jeremiah 1:5 for the rest of you." These ladies glanced at each other knowingly. Some of Paul's readers would have had the same grasp of the Scriptures; they like these grandmothers were seasoned and experienced exegetes.

Paul didn't twist Scripture, but he did squeeze every drop out of it. Paul himself was so familiar with Scripture—with the full scope and subtle nuances, with the historical patterns of Israel's history—that he was able to use these advanced tools faithfully to open the true revelation of God's promises for all people in all generations.

Conclusion

SHOULD WE BE FOLLOWING PAUL?

We haven't covered all the accusations leveled at Paul. Some scholars have argued that Paul taught a different gospel than Jesus proclaimed. Jesus preached about the kingdom of heaven, but Paul seldom mentioned it. We have lots of stories of Jesus that begin with "The kingdom of heaven is like a . . . ." Paul might mention that such and such kind of person won't inherit the kingdom of God, but the kingdom is not a theme in Paul's teaching like it is in the preaching of Jesus. Paul preached, "If you declare with your mouth, 'Jesus is Lord,' and believe in your heart that God raised him from the dead, you will be saved." (Rom 10:9). In fact, Paul wrote, "For Christ is the end of the law so that there may be righteousness for everyone who believes" (Rom 10:4 NRSV), whereas Jesus announced, "Do not think that I have come to abolish the Law or the Prophets; I have not come to abolish them but to fulfill them. For truly I tell you, until heaven and earth disappear, not the smallest letter, not the least stroke of a pen, will by any means disappear from the Law until everything is accomplished" (Mt 5:17-18).

Some have suggested Jesus was an itinerant preacher, calling the nation of Israel back to faithfulness. And then Paul turned this Galilean preacher into a Greco-Roman religion, inventing "Christianity." Much ink has been spilled in the last hundred years over this topic. The issue is technically described as the challenge of determining the continuity from Jesus to Paul. Obviously, their messages aren't exactly the same, yet we see no reason for the skeptical view that Paul broke from Jesus and created a Greco-Roman savior religion that we term Christianity. First, Paul preached from hindsight. The preaching of Jesus occurred *before* the cross and resurrection. The redemption of humanity through Christ had not yet occurred. Second, there actually are connections between Jesus and Paul. Many scholars today suggest that Paul "unpacked" the implications of the message of Jesus. Just as Stephen (in Acts 6–8) understood the ramifications of the good news of Jesus, so also did Paul. While Peter and John are still going to the temple to pray (Acts 3:1-9), both Stephen and Paul understood that the role of the temple would change under the new covenant. In the decades that followed, other voices joined theirs (Heb 8), and we finally see Peter understanding as well (1 Pet 2).

All this is to say Paul didn't invent (or reinvent) Christianity; he contextualized it. In fact, he contextualized it for specific congregations in specific cultures. When we read Paul's letters to the Corinthians or Thessalonians, we are reading his teachings on how to live faithfully as a Christian in Corinth or Thessalonica. Paul understood that one size doesn't fit all. The correct guidance for one church may be different than for another. As we have already argued, you can have different rules for different folks. This isn't inconsistency. It is contextualization. Paul was aware of the ditch on both sides of the road. Those about to stray into the ditch on the right, such as legalism, need to be encouraged that the Christian life is more than rules like "Do not handle! Do not taste! Do not touch!" (Col 2:21). We have freedom in Christ. But to those about to fall in the ditch on the other side, using freedom as a rationalization for sin, Paul has a different word: "Do not let sin reign in your mortal body" (Rom 6:12) or "But now you must also rid yourselves of all such things as these: anger, rage, malice, slander, and filthy language from your lips. Do not lie to each other, since you have taken off your old self with its practices" (Col 3:8-9). Paul isn't talking out of both sides of his mouth. He is contextualizing the same message, the Christian message, to two different groups.

Knocking Paul Off His Pedestal

The purpose of this book has not been to hate on Paul. He's a hero of ours. We've dedicated our lives to studying his writings and to teaching new Christians to imitate Paul. But we have tried to describe Paul in more realistic terms because we all need a more flesh-and-blood Paul and less of a super-spiritualized Paul-on-a-Pedestal. The superhuman Paul can't be imitated. We sometimes create an image of Paul that makes him just a notch below Jesus. So when Paul said, "Imitate me" (1 Cor 4:16), we think, *Good grief, that's impossible.* But Paul didn't intend it to be. He was aware of his own failings. Luke also wanted us to know that Paul was a regular human.

Luke told two stories about Paul where his readers would have known that Paul was *wrong*. Luke tells us that Paul argued with Barnabas over John Mark. Barnabas thought John Mark was a keeper, but Paul had washed his hands of him, viewing John Mark as a quitter (Acts 15:36-41). Yet, Luke's readers knew the story of John Mark—the man wrote a Gospel! In a later story,

Luke tells us that Paul told the Ephesians that they would never see him again (Acts 20:25) and that he thought the Spirit wanted him to go to Jerusalem (Acts 20:22). Luke then tells us at least twice that the Spirit was telling Paul *not* to go (Acts 21:4, 11-12). Luke's readers know the Jerusalem visit was a disaster. They also know that Paul later visited the Ephesians again, even leaving Timothy there to minister (1 Tim 1:3). Luke wants us to know that Paul was no god or divine-man. Sure, Paul was used by the Spirit (in mighty ways) but he was still a mortal human.

When the folks in Lystra tried to put Paul and Barnabas on a pedestal, he cried out, "Friends, why are you doing this? We too are only human, like you" (Acts 14:15). The Lystrans wanted Paul on a pedestal. For Christians, only Jesus is to be worshiped. We should strive to imitate Paul, but a mortal, human Paul.

Because the Bible is so very relevant to most of our lives, we can easily forget that it is an ancient document. We are often guilty of holding Paul up to twenty-first-century standards. But Paul would make a lousy American: he was often "politically incorrect" and he *usually* talked about religion and politics.

Paul was a product of his time—like everybody else. When biographers tells the stories of Abraham Lincoln or Mahatma Gandhi, they usually begin by explaining the culture and times. This helps explain the "givens" of the culture, the contexts of what was happening. Sure, Lincoln was able to transcend his time; Gandhi reached beyond his culture. Paul does the same. Understanding people's time and culture tells us more about their starting point than their ending point, but it is the proper place to start.

Do We Imitate Paul?

How do we imitate a man who sometimes behaved badly? Paul was willing to speak out even if his view was unpopular with the broader culture or with the views of religious folks. Paul wouldn't allow the wealthy to have extra privileges. Even a patroness who was paying all the bills and hosting the house church had to learn quietly like the others, even the slaves. Imitating Paul may require taking an unpopular position.

On the other hand, Paul wasn't a jerk or a hypocrite and we shouldn't be either. Paul's writings possess a nuance that we can easily miss. He claims and uses his Roman citizenship but then tells the Philippians that it isn't worth anything compared to Christ. But this wasn't talking out of both sides of his mouth. We need to read deeply and understand what was going on. Those who accuse Paul of lying and manipulating are usually pulling his statements out of context or failing to understand the subtleties of the situation.

Did Paul behave badly? Well, yes. Sometimes he didn't behave like his culture wanted nor like ours wants him to behave today. When Paul denounced homosexual practice for both the active as well as the passive partner, he was behaving badly in Roman eyes. But when he welcomed both into the church as sinners in need of a savior (like the rest of us), he was behaving badly in Jewish eyes. Paul did indeed behave badly in the eyes of his culture and sometimes even in the eyes of other Christians. When we hold a stance like Paul's, we may well find ourselves, like Paul, denounced by both the culture and the Pharisees. Paul was not willing to "blend in" or "go with the flow" or "go along to get along" when it came to the truth of the gospel. He wasn't interested in riding the latest cultural wave and he wasn't afraid of being on the wrong side of popular thought. Paul wasn't in step with either his Jewish or Roman culture. The church may never get to where Paul dreamed it could be—the spotless bride of Christ—but Paul will always push us.

The old phrase "The gospel comforts the afflicted and afflicts the comfortable" describes well the gospel Paul preached. The man who encouraged Christians to "live peaceful and quiet lives" (1 Tim 2:2) was the same one who could throw a city into an uproar (Acts 16:20). Paul knew when an uproar was needed for the sake of the truth of the gospel and was willing to pay the price:

> Five times I received from the Jews the forty lashes minus one. Three times I was beaten with rods, once I was pelted with stones, three times I was shipwrecked, I spent a night and a day in the open sea, I have been constantly on the move. I have been in danger from rivers, in danger from bandits, in danger from my fellow Jews, in danger from Gentiles; in danger in the city, in danger in the country, in danger at sea; and in danger from false believers. I have labored and toiled and have often gone without sleep; I have known hunger and thirst and have often gone without food; I have been cold and naked. Besides everything else, I face daily the pressure of my concern for all the churches. (2 Cor 11:24-28)

This piece of autobiography contains a word of caution: if we stand with Paul against both culture and the Pharisees among us, we have to also be ready to pay the price.

Paul may have been more stubborn than we like, but he's the same guy who dusted himself off and marched right back into a town where people had just stoned him for preaching the gospel. Pioneering spirit and political correctness rarely go together. We might not want to share a cubicle with Paul or let him speak at our church business meeting. He might cause us to wince on occasion. He often embarrasses us in front of our non-Christian friends. He can even be a bull in a china shop at times, but he's the one we want championing our cause. And we want to imitate him as he imitated Christ.

ACKNOWLEDGMENTS

We want to thank InterVarsity Press for suggesting that we tackle this project. We thank our wives for the extra load they bear so we can make the time we need to write. We thank our friends who previewed chapters of this book and made them better before we send them to print, especially Anthony Hendricks, Joey Dodson and Daniel Cathers. We also need to thank Jesse Grenz, a promising young scholar, who prepared the indexes, looked up references and ran other errands with a cheerful spirit and a gracious heart. Lastly, we thank our fellow ministers and church members, past and present, who challenged us to look at Paul with fresh eyes, to appreciate him in his culture as well as ours and to renew our commitment to imitate Paul as he imitated Christ.

NOTES

Introduction: The Problems with Paul

[1]Albert Schweitzer, *The Mysticism of Paul the Apostle*, repr. ed. (New York, Seabury, 1968), 171. Emphasis added.

[2]David Dubuque, "Unlike Jesus, 'St. Paul' Put Down the Weak: Women, Jews, Gays, Slaves, and the Poor," accessed May 12, 2016, www.liberals likechrist.org/+Believable/PaulvsAll-1.html.

[3]For more background on the life of Paul, see, e.g., David Capes, Rodney Reeves and E. Randolph Richards, *Rediscovering Paul* (Downers Grove, IL: InterVarsity Press, 2007).

[4]Clearly, we can't know Paul's daily calendar, but he does quote Greek playwrights (1 Cor 15:33) and uses illustrations from the games (1 Cor 9:24-26); Corinth had a theater and hosted the Isthmian Games.

1 Paul Was Kind of a Jerk

[1]Gerd Lüdemann, "Paul, the Promoter of Christianity," December 2014, www.bibleinterp.com/articles/2014/12/lud388017.shtml.

[2]Femi Aribisala, "Paul: The Hypocritical Pharisee," *Premium Times Nigeria*, June 16, 2013, www.premiumtimesng.com/opinion/138853-article-of -faith-paul-the-hypocritical-pharisee-by-femi-aribisala.html.

[3]Lüdemann, "Paul."

[4]Not all agree. Many scholars just can't bring themselves to say that Paul was wrong. For example, D. A. Carson (following Wayne Grudem) interprets Acts 21:4 this way: "These prophets had received some revelation about the apostle's impending sufferings, and *interpreted* them to mean Paul should not go," Carson, *Showing the Spirit: A Theological Exposition of 1 Corinthians 12-14* (Grand Rapids: Baker Academic, 1996), 97. But Luke doesn't describe it as two interpretations of what the Spirit said.

[5]See Craig Keener, *Acts: An Exegetical Commentary* (Grand Rapids: Baker Academic, 2014), 3:3135-3138, for a very full description of the issues and options for the vow.

[6]Craig Keener, *The IVP Bible Background Commentary: New Testament*, 2nd ed. (Downers Grove, IL: InterVarsity Press, 2014), 386.

[7]Likely Paul assumed that in seven days he would wash his hands of Jerusalem and go on to Spain. Paul's opponents, however, exploit the situation, since they now know exactly when Paul would next visit the temple. They use the intervening days of the vow to build opposition in order to start a riot in the temple. Paul is nearly killed and his planned trip to Spain is delayed at least four years. There is no hint James or the Jerusalem church was involved in this plot.

[8]See David Capes, Rodney Reeves and E. Randolph Richards, *Rediscovering Paul* (Downers Grove, IL: InterVarsity Press, 2007), 29-33. For a more general discussion of honor and shame, see Richards and Brandon J. O'Brien, *Misreading Scripture with Western Eyes* (Downers Grove, IL: InterVarsity Press, 2012), 116-35.

[9]Rodney Reeves, *Spirituality According to Paul: Imitating the Apostle of Christ* (Downers Grove, IL: InterVarsity Press, 2011), 15-16.

[10]See for example, Capes, Reeves and Richards, *Rediscovering Paul*, 42-47.

[11]Martin Luther, *Commentary on Galatians* (1538; repr., Wheaton, IL: Crossway, 1998), 219.

[12]Scholars call these "tribulation lists." These were yet another subtle sign of Paul's rhetorical skill, of which the Corinthians had asserted Paul had little. He is countering their accusation without directly confronting them. See E. Randolph Richards, *The Secretary in the Letters of Paul*, WUNT 2/42 (Tübingen: Mohr Siebeck, 1991), 209-10.

2 Paul Was a Killjoy

[1]Charles Haddon Spurgeon, *Illustrations and Meditations: Flowers from a Puritan's Garden*. London: Passmore & Alabaster, 1883.

[2]Ibid.

[3]Ibid.

[4]In fairness, Paul's first list is of things the Colossians have already put off (more or less) and the second list is of vices Paul now wants them to address. Still, there are twice as many. Paul follows traditional rhetorical practice and lists five (with a summary vice or virtue) for each list. See E. Randolph Richards, "Stop Lying," *Biblical Illustrator* (Spring 1999): 77-80.

[5]Titus Livius (Livy), *The History of Rome*, 39.13.10-11, ed. and trans., Evan T. Sage, Loeb Classical Library (Cambridge, MA: Harvard University Press, 1936), 255.

[6]Athenagoras of Athens, *Legatio pro Christianis* 3-4, trans. B. P. Pratten,

accessed July 12, 2015, www.earlychristianwritings.com/text/athenagoras-plea.html.

[7]Ibid.

[8]Tertullian, *Apologeticus* 7.1, trans. by T. R. Glover and Gerald H. Rendell, Loeb Classical Library (Cambridge, MA: Harvard University Press, 1931), p. 37. He complains that some Christians were tortured to find out "how many murdered babies each of us has tasted" (2.5), 10.

[9]For a good discussion of *convivia* and the association with Corinth, see Ben Witherington III, *Conflict and Community in Corinth: A Socio-Rhetorical Commentary on 1 and 2 Corinthians* (Grand Rapids: Eerdmans, 1995), esp. 193-99.

3 Paul Was a Racist

[1]Martin Luther, *On the Jews and Their Lies*, Part V.

[2]All works by Epimenides (ca. 600 BC) are lost but this quote is known by other ancients citing him. Did Epimenides hate on his own people? It wasn't until the Middle Ages that scholars began noticing the logical paradox. Epimenides starts by saying that all Cretans (which included him) are liars. If they are liars, then he is lying when he says they are lazy sluggards and gluttons. Most folks missed the paradox for hundreds of years. We certainly can't fault Paul for not getting it either.

[3]Jerome Murphy-O'Connor, *Paul: A Critical Life* (Oxford: Clarendon, 1996), 189-90

[4]Stephen Mitchell, *Anatolia: Land, Men, and Gods of Asia Minor, vol. 2, The Rise of the Church* (Oxford: Clarendon, 1995), 4.

[5]Like just about everything else in Pauline studies, this is debated. In the last ten years, there is increasing movement to prefer *Judean* over *Jew*. See, e.g., Frederick W. Danker, *"Ioudaios,"* in *A Greek-English Lexicon of the New Testament and Other Early Christian Literature*, 3rd ed. (Chicago: University of Chicago Press, 2001). The venerable *Cambridge History of Judaism* added "Judean" as a fourth optional meaning in its 1999 edition (vol. 3, p. 210). This meaning is gaining acceptance faster among Jewish scholars than Christian ones; see Daniel R. Schwartz, *Judeans and Jews: Four Faces of Dichotomy in Ancient Jewish History* (Toronto: University of Toronto Press, 2014). The article by Steve Mason is often cited as seminal: "Jews, Judaeans, Judaizing, Judaism: Problems of Categorization in Ancient History," *Journal for the Study of Judaism* 38 (2007): 457-512.

[6]Several inscriptions (about 150 BC) from the Greek island of Delos mention these "Israelites" who sacrifice at the Samaritan temple, Donald D. Binder, "Delos," Second Temple Synagogues, accessed January 27, 2016, http://www.pohick.org/sts/delos.html. Some Jewish scholars dispute the identification of the building as a synagogue or even the Israelites as Israelites, e.g., Lidia Matassa, "Unraveling the Myth of the Synagogue on Delos," *Bulletin of the Anglo-Israel Archaeological Society* 25 (2007): 81-115.

It is popular in some church circles today to ascribe the origins of the Samaritan people to intermarriage between Jews and Assyrians after the destruction of the Northern Kingdom in 722 BC, labeling them derogatorily as "half-breeds" who also mixed their religions. Judeans in Jesus' day clearly did not like the Samaritans. When heaping insults on Jesus, Judeans called him "demon-possessed" and a "Samaritan" (Jn 8:48). Since the Judeans are clearly biased, most scholars do not accept their version of the story uncritically. (The Bible says almost nothing about Samaritan origins.) Currently, it is thought Samaritans gradually parted ways with the rest of the Israelites over centuries, with the building of the rival temple to God (Yahweh) in 332 BC as the watershed moment. See Wayne Brindle, "The Origin and History of the Samaritans," *Grace Theological Seminary* 5.1 (1984): 47-75, or Magnar Kartveit, *The Origins of the Samaritans*, VTSup 128 (Leiden: Brill, 2009).

[7]Petronius, *Poems*, 97, trans. M. Heseltine and W. H. D. Rouse, rev. E. H. Warmington, Loeb Classical Library (Cambridge, MA: Harvard University Press, 1975), p. 425.

[8]See the excellent discussion by J. Daniel Hays. He also connects it to Moses' second wife and the implications against common American racism; Hays, *From Every People and Nation: A Biblical Theology of Race*, New Studies in Biblical Theology 14 (Downers Grove, IL: InterVarsity Press, 2003), esp. 70-81.

[9]See the excellent discussion by Luke Timothy Johnson, *The First and Second Letters to Timothy*, vol. 35A of *The Anchor Bible* (New York: Doubleday, 2001), 137-42.

[10]Again, this interpretation is debated.

4 Paul Supported Slavery

[1]Frederick Douglass, *Narrative of the Life of Frederick Douglass, an American Slave*. (Barnes and Noble Classics: New York, 2003), 55-57.

Douglass was himself a Christian and had a nuanced view of the way religion was used to support both slavery and abolition.

[2]Ebenezer W. Warren. *Nellie Norton: or, Southern slavery and the Bible: a Scriptural refutation of the principal arguments upon which the abolitionists rely. A vindication of Southern slavery from the Old and New Testaments* (Macon, GA.: Burke, Boykin & Co., 1864), 11.

[3]Kimberley Flint-Hamilton, "Images of Slavery in the Early Church: Hatred Disguised as Love?," *Journal of Hate Studies* 2 (2003): 27-45, esp. 31-33.

[4]Galen estimated the slave population in Pergamum to be 25 percent, *De propriorum animi cuiuslibet affectuum dignotione* 9.13; see W. V. Harris, "Demography, Geography and the Sources of Roman Slaves," *The Journal of Roman Studies* 89 (1999): 62-75, esp. 65.

[5]C. Osiek, "Slavery in the New Testament World," *Bible Today* 22:3 (May 1984): 151.

[6]See for example, J. Scott Bartchy, *First-Century Slavery and the Interpretation of 1 Corinthians 7:21* (Eugene, OR: Wipf and Stock, 2003), 41.

[7]Paleodemographics is a tricky and complicated field. Philosophical writings were too idealistic. The deaths of infants and the elderly was probably underreported. Scientific methods for accurately ageing adult bones are disputed. Tomb inscriptions, if reliable, remain one of the better methods. See Walter Scheidel, "Disease and Death in the Ancient City of Rome," (Princeton/Stanford Working Papers in Classics Stanford University, Stanford, CA, April 2009): 1-14, esp. 6, www.princeton.edu/~pswpc/pdfs/scheidel/040901.pdf.

[8]A plague was ravaging Rome in AD 65, while Paul was awaiting execution: "a plague which in a single autumn entered thirty thousand deaths," Suetonius, *Lives of Caesar* 2: *Nero,* trans. J. C. Rolfe, Loeb Classical Library (Cambridge, MA: Harvard University Press, 1914), 151. Rodney Stark, *The Rise of Christianity: How the Obscure, Marginal Jesus Movement Became the Dominant Religious Force in the Western World in a Few Centuries* (San Francisco: Harper, 1997), paints a fairly terrifying picture of life in the Roman Empire.

[9]The laws governing the status of the children, though, were complicated. Ibid., 115.

[10]See R. H. Barrow, *Slavery in the Roman Empire* (London: Methuen, 1928), 170-71.

[11]Seneca, *Epistles,* 47.2-3.

[12]Timothy A. Brookins, "(Dis)Correspondence of Paul and Seneca on Slavery: a Sociological Perspective," in *Paul and Seneca in Dialogue,* eds. David Briones and Joseph Dodson, New Testament and Ancient Philosophy Series (Leiden: Brill, forthcoming), 3. We are heavily indebted to Brookins's many insights in this excellent essay and we are grateful to him for allowing us to see a prepublication draft.

[13]Sen., *Ep.* 47.7.

[14]Sen., *Ep.* 47.1

[15]Sen., *Ep.* 47.10.

[16]Seneca, *De Brevitate Vitae.* 5.3.

[17]Sen. *Ep.* 47.17.

[18]See Brookins, "(Dis)Correspondence," 22.

[19]Bob Dylan, vocal performance of "Gotta Serve Somebody," *Slow Train Coming,* 1979, Sony Records.

[20]Brookins, "(Dis)Correspondence," 18.

[21]Ibid., 20. The paraphrase of Ephesians 6:5-9 is his, capturing Paul's "do the same things to them."

[22]Sen., *Ep.* 47.10.

[23]Sen., *Ep.* 47.16.

[24]See the wonderful contrast between Paul and Seneca in Brookins, "(Dis) Correspondence," esp. 10.

[25]Brookins, "(Dis)Correspondence," 33.

[26]Thus, the argument of Brookins, "(Dis)Correspondence."

5 Paul Was a Chauvinist

[1]Jemima Thackray, "We Christians Must Face It: The Bible Is Hugely Misogynistic," *The Telegraph,* February 13, 2014, www.telegraph.co.uk /women/womens-life/10635510/Women-bishops-We-Christians-need -to-face-up-to-facts-about-Bible.html.

[2]Sarah Grimké, *Letters on the Equality of the Sexes, and the Condition of Woman: Addressed to Mary S. Parker* (Boston, MA: I. Knapp, 1838), 10.

[3]Lynn Cohick, *Women in the World of the Earliest Christians: Illuminating Ancient Ways of Life* (Grand Rapids: Baker Academic, 2009), 69.

[4]Livy, *Hist.* 1.57.6-58; see Cohick, *Women,* 69-70.

[5]Cohick, *Women,* 180.

[6]Ruth A. Tucker and Walter Liefeld, *Daughters of the Church: Women and Ministry from the New Testament Times to the Present* (Grand

Rapids: Zondervan, 1987), 56. Tucker and Liefeld's entire chapter 2 ("Acts and Epistles") is very helpful for historical context. We also recommend Bruce Winter, *Roman Wives, Roman Widows: The Appearance of New Women and the Pauline Communities* (Grand Rapids: Eerdmans, 2003).

[7]Cohick, *Women*, 180.

[8]Josephus, *C. Ap.* 2.201, trans. H. St. John Thackeray.

[9]Craig S. Keener, *Paul, Women and Wives: Marriage and Women's Ministry in the Letters of Paul* (Peabody, MA: Hendrickson, 1992). 114. We are indebted to Keener for the illustrations as well.

[10]See, for example, the excellent discussion by Keener on the first two issues (church and family) in *Paul, Women and Wives.*

[11]Dio Chrysostom, *Or.* 64.3.

[12]William J. Martin, "1 Corinthians 11:2-26: An Interpretation," in W. Ward Gasque and R. P. Martin, eds., *Apostolic History and the Gospel: Biblical and Historical Essays Presented to F. F. Bruce*, 232-42 (Peabody: Hendrickson, 1992), 234.

[13]Bruce Winter, *After Paul Left Corinth* (Grand Rapids: Eerdmans, 2001), 128.

[14]E. Randolph Richards and Brandon J. O'Brien, *Misreading Scripture with Western Eyes* (Downers Grove, IL: InterVarsity Press, 2012) 43-44.

[15]Tucker and Liefeld, *Daughters of the Church*, 60.

[16]Isoc., *Demon.* 41; *Or.*, 1; see Keener, *Paul, Women and Wives*, 107-8.

[17]*m. 'Abot*, 3:14; see Aída Besançon Spencer, *Beyond the Curse: Women Called to Ministry*, repr. ed. (Peabody, MA: Hendrickson, 1989), 78.

[18]Quoted in Andrew B. McGowan, *Ancient Christian Worship: Early Church Practices in Social, Historical, and Theological Perspective* (Grand Rapids: Baker Academic, 2014), 69. Emphasis added.

[19]Keener, *Paul, Women and Wives*, 108.

[20]Quintilian, *The Institutio Oratoria of Quintilian* 1.3-4, trans. H. E. Butler, Loeb Classical Library (Cambridge, MA: Harvard University Press, 1920), 59. Emphasis added.

[21]William Stearns Davis, *A Day in Old Athens* (Cheshire, CT: Biblo-Moser, 1960), 52.

[22]Bruce Winter, *Roman Wives, Roman Widows: The Appearance of New Women and the Pauline Communities* (Grand Rapids: Eerdmans, 2003), esp. 77-172.

[23]Some rabbis also noted that Eve was deceived at least partly because she received the commandment secondhand; see Keener, *Paul, Women and Wives,* 115.

[24]See, *e.g.,* Cohick, *Women*; Stanley Grenz and Denise Muir Kjesbo, *Women in the Church: A Biblical Theology of Women in Ministry* (Downers Grove: InterVarsity Press, 1995); Bonnidell Clouse and Robert Clouse, eds., *Women in Ministry: Four Views* (Downers Grove: InterVarsity Press, 1989); Carolyn Osiek, Margaret MacDonald and Janet Tulloch, *A Woman's Place: House Churches in Earliest Christianity* (Minneapolis: Fortress Press, 2006); as well as Keener, *Paul, Women and Wives;* and Spencer, *Curse.*

[25]In fact, there are several other tough exegetical issues in 1 Timothy 2 and in Paul's other passages, but we do not have the space to cover them. Again, we would commend a more detailed study, such as Keener, *Paul, Women and Wives* or the balanced presentation of the two major evangelical positions on the subject, Beck, *Two Views.*

[26]For a more technical exegesis, see, for example, Spencer, *Curse,* esp. 92. She notes Ignatius, *Eph.* 19.1. Also, Paul states Jesus was "born of woman" (Gal 4:4).

[27]If Roman culture had the movement that Bruce Winter terms "the new Roman women," these women were going much further than even Paul by casting off moral constraints and other behaviors and views. This movement did *not* become the new Roman standard. Paul spoke out in opposition to it, as did Romans (and presumably Jews). As a countercultural, minority movement, this would be a separate trajectory analysis.

[28]This conclusion is scarcely original to us. This is the conclusion of William Webb, the pioneer of the trajectory hermeneutic, *Slaves, Women and Homosexuals: Exploring the Hermeneutics of Cultural Analysis* (Downers Grove, IL: InterVarsity Press, 2001).

[29]Some writers would want to point out that these two women weren't getting along as well as Paul wanted (Phil 4:2), but that is true of plenty of men in Paul's letters. In fact, male workers in general get harsher rebukes from Paul.

[30]The "new women" in the movement springing up in Roman culture, who were casting off moral constraints and shirking responsibilities, would not have approved of Paul either. They would have viewed him, as some critics do today, as a relic of a dying past. See Bruce Winter description of this subculture during Paul's day, *Roman Wives*; Cohick cautions that

the Augustinian laws prohibiting such behaviors may not be signs of a true movement but rather a straw man that Augustus creates to help underscore the importance of traditional woman values. Either way, it shows the traditional Roman image of woman was the prevalent view; see Cohick, *Women*, 72-75.

[31]Sarah Grimké, *Letters on the Equality of the Sexes*, 60.

6 Paul Was Homophobic

[1]Jonathan Parnell, "Why Homosexuality Is Not Like Other Sins," *Desiring God* (website), April 21, 2014, www.desiringgod.org/articles/why-homo sexuality-is-not-like-other-sins.

[2]Elizabeth Dias, "How Evangelicals Are Changing Their Minds on Gay Marriage," *Time*, January 15, 2015, time.com/3669024/evangelicals-gay -marriage.

[3]Lucretius, *De Rerum Natura* 4.1055-1056. That Lucretius means sexual contact and not some vague notion of love is clear: "he . . . desires to unite and to cast fluid from body to body," 4.1057, 358-59).

[4]See Elizabeth Manwell, "Gender and Masculinity," in *A Companion to Catullus*, ed. Marilyn Skinner, Blackwell Companions to the Ancient World (Malden, MA: Blackwell Publishing, 2011), 117-118.

[5]Juvenal, *Satire* 6.25-37 (LCL 91:236-237). Forgive the unpleasant crassness, but we want you to see what this public and widely acclaimed work described. Again, those who say our culture is more accepting than Paul's culture have simply not read enough.

[6]In a lesser known work by the Roman poet Martial, *Epigrams* 11.6, the poet encourages his young cupbearer Dindymus: "Boy, mix me bumpers half [wine] and half [water], such as Pythagorus used to give to Nero, mix them, Dindymus, and not too long between them . . . Give me kisses, Catullian kisses. If they shall be as many as he said, 'I will give you Catullus' Sparrow.'" The meaning of the poem is unfortunately clear; see Edward Champlin, *Nero* (Cambridge, MA: Belknap Press, 2005), 169: "Wine and kisses will so arouse the poet that he will give the boy his *passer* [sparrow], referring to his genitals. "*Passer* can have this lewd meaning, and the name of the cupbearer, 'Dindymus,' confirms the obscenity. . . . Elsewhere in his epigrams Martial employs the name to refer to passive, effeminate males, objects of either the poet's ridicule or his lust."

[7]Amy Richlin, *The Garden of Priapus: Sexuality and Aggression in Roman Humor* (Oxford: Oxford University Press, 1992), 225.

[8]Michael Ehrhardt, "Wrestling with Greco-Roman Mores: An Interview with Charles Rowan Beye," *Gay & Lesbian Review Worldwide* 20, no. 3 (May/Jun 2013): 34. Emphasis added.

[9]Tac., *Ann.* 15.37.

[10]See for example, Craig Williams, *Roman Homosexuality,* 2nd ed. (Oxford: Oxford University Press, 2009), 6. Romans used lots of terms but to demean, not to indicate a sexual orientation.

[11]See Richlin, *Garden*, 225.

[12]Thus, Suetonius shames Nero for sleeping with freeborn boys, married women, a vestal virgin, a freedwoman *and* for taking the submissive role with a man; Suet., *Nero* 6.28.

[13]Richlin, *Garden,* 225.

[14]Amy Richlin, "Not Before Homosexuality: The Materiality of the Cinaedus and the Roman Law against Love Between Men," *Journal of the History of Sexuality* 3/4 (1993): 523-573, 531.

[15]Williams, *Roman Homosexuality,* 199: "No one seems to have called a man's desire to penetrate a lovely boy a *morbus.*" Homosexual desire wasn't considered a disease. Rather, a man's desire to take the receptive role was termed "sick."

[16]Webb prefers to describe his method as a "redemptive-movement hermeneutic." He notes, "some may prefer calling this interpretive/applicational approach a 'progressive' or 'developmental' or 'trajectory' hermeneutic," William Webb, *Slaves, Women, and Homosexuals: Exploring the Hermeneutics of Cultural Analysis* (Downers Grove: InterVarsity Press, 2001), 31.

[17]Ibid., 88.

7 Paul Was a Hypocrite

[1]Femi Aribisala, "Paul: The Hypocritical Pharisee, Article of Faith" *Premium Times Nigeria,* June 16, 2013, www.premiumtimesng.com/opinion/138853-article-of-faith-paul-the-hypocritical-pharisee-by-femi-aribisala.html.

[2]We are indebted to Winter's insightful discussion of Paul and meat markets, Bruce Winter, *After Paul Left Corinth: The Influence of Secular Ethics and Social Change* (Grand Rapids: Eerdmans, 2001), 287-301.

[3]Winter, *After Paul Left Corinth,* 288-89.

[4]So argues Winter, 297.

[5]John Barclay recently published what promises to be a landmark study on "gift" in the ancient world, noting that gifts had strings attached, *Paul and the Gift* (Grand Rapids: Eerdmans, 2015). Barclay argues the ancient system of gift giving is central to understanding Paul's theology. See, also, the excellent study by David E. Briones, *Paul's Financial Policy: A Socio-Theological Approach,* Library of New Testament Studies 494 (London: Bloomsbury, 2013).

[6]Sen., *On Benefits* 2.18.5.

[7]See Randolph Richards, "Flattery, Favors, and Obligations: Patrons and Clients in Greco-Roman Culture," *Biblical Illustrator* (Spring 2011): 26-29.

[8]The dating of Galatians is debated, but we are following the common evangelical reconstruction where Galatians was Paul's first letter.

[9]See Mark Nanos, "Was Paul a 'Liar' for the Gospel?: The Case for a New Interpretation of Paul's 'Becoming Everything to Everyone' in 1 Corinthians 9:19-23," *Review & Expositor* 110.4 (2013): 591-608.

[10]Ovid, Metamorphosis 8.626-724; to understand the connection to the Acts story, see for example, David Peterson, *The Acts of the Apostles,* Pillar New Testament Commentary (Grand Rapids: Eerdmans, 2009), 408.

8 Paul Twisted Scripture

[1]Before you get too defensive, read our explanation in E. Randolph Richards and Brandon J. O'Brien, *Misreading Scripture with Western Eyes* (Downers Grove, IL: InterVarsity Press, 2013), 199-202.

[2]Gordon Fee and Douglas Stuart explain each of these steps ably in *How To Read the Bible for All Its Worth,* 4th ed. (Grand Rapids: Zondervan, 2014). An equally great resource is Duvall and Hays, *Grasping God's Word,* 3rd ed. (Grand Rapids: Zondervan, 2012).

[3]Leroy Huizenga, "St. Paul Would Have Failed My Hermeneutics Course," *First Things,* July 28, 2011, www.firstthings.com/web-exclusives/2011/07/st-paul-would-have-failed-my-hermeneutics-course.

[4]Peter Enns, "Would Paul Have Made a Good Evangelical?" May 24, 2012, www.patheos.com/blogs/peterenns/2012/05/would-paul-have-made-a-good-evangelical.

[5]Richard N. Longenecker, *Biblical Exegesis in the Apostolic Period,* 2nd ed. (Grand Rapids: Eerdmans, 1999), 106-7.

[6]See, for example, Carol K. Stockhausen, "2 Corinthians 3 and the Principles of Pauline Exegesis," in *Paul and the Scriptures of Israel,* ed. C. A. Evans and J. A. Sanders, vol. 83 of JSNTSup, (Sheffield: Sheffield Academic, 1993), 143-64, esp. 144-46.

[7]See, e.g., Ps. Philo, *Biblical Antiquities* 10.7.

[8]*b Mak* 16a. We are indebted to Longenecker, *Biblical Exegesis,* 99-100, for this and the other examples of pearl stringing. We have added the emphasis to show the strung pearls.

[9]See George Guthrie, *The Structure of Hebrews: A Text-Linguistic Analysis,* Biblical Studies Library (Grand Rapids: Baker Books, 1994). Guthrie calls the strung pearls "hook words." To see how this analysis impacts exegesis, see George Guthrie, *Hebrews,* The NIV Application Commentary (Grand Rapids: Zondervan, 1998).

[10]See, for example, the careful study by Linda Belleville, *Reflections of Glory: Paul's Polemical Use of the Moses-Doxa Tradition in 2 Corinthians 3:1-18* vol. 52 of JSNTSup (Sheffield: Sheffield Academic, 1991).

[11]Origen, "Homilies on Exodus, V." in *Homilies on Genesis and Exodus,* trans. by Roland Heine (1982), 275.

[12]Ibid., 277.

[13]John Calvin, *Galatians, Ephesians, Philippians, and Colossians,* trans. T. H. L. Parker, vol. 11 of *Calvin's New Testament Commentaries* (Grand Rapids: Eerdmans, 1996), 84.

[14]An excellent scholar on this topic is David B. Capes, *Old Testament Yahweh Texts in Paul's Christology,* WUNT 2/47 (Tübingen: Mohr Siebeck, 1992).

[15]Plato, *Phaedrus,* trans. Harold N. Fowler, Loeb Classical Library 36 (Cambridge: Harvard University Press, 1914), p. 563.

[16]See for example, Richard Hess and E. Randolph Richards, eds., *Read Scripture Deeply* (Charleston: CreateSpace, 2015).

AUTHOR INDEX

SUBJECT INDEX

SCRIPTURE INDEX